BIRDIE

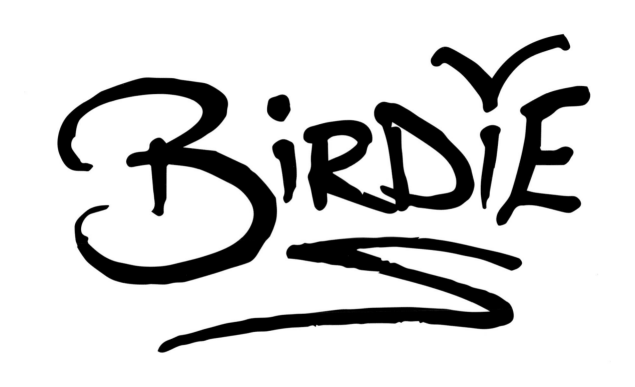

THE BEST OF BIRDIE

Published in 2015 by Racing Post Books

27 Kingfisher Court, Hambridge Road
Newbury, RG14 5SJ

10 9 8 7 6 5 4 3 2 1

A catalogue record for this book is available from the British Library.

ISBN 978-1-910498-14-9

Designed by J. Schwartz & Co.

Printed and bound in the Czech Republic by Finidr

Every effort has been made to fulfil requirements with regard to copyright material. The author and publisher will be glad to rectify any omissions at the earliest opportunity.

www.racingpost.com/shop

To friends old and
new, my family and
those special few.
Thank you for all your
fantastic support and
making my dream
come true.

BIRDIE is set to become a name and a cartoon style no one will forget.

Darren 'Birdie' Bird has quickly established himself with his brilliant, quirky cartoons on all aspects of the racing game whilst pursuing his day job as Force Artist with Suffolk Police, where his 'art' includes everything from posters for Christmas socials to 'E-Fits' of crime suspects.

'Birdie' started by putting his cartoons out on social media but was picked up by Channel 4 Racing and used on every day of the 2014 Cheltenham Festival. His unique take on the racing scene has seen his work sought after by private commissions, readers of the *Racing Post* and any punter with half a grain of humour in the soul.

This first book is unlikely to be his last.

BROUGH SCOTT
Racing Post Books

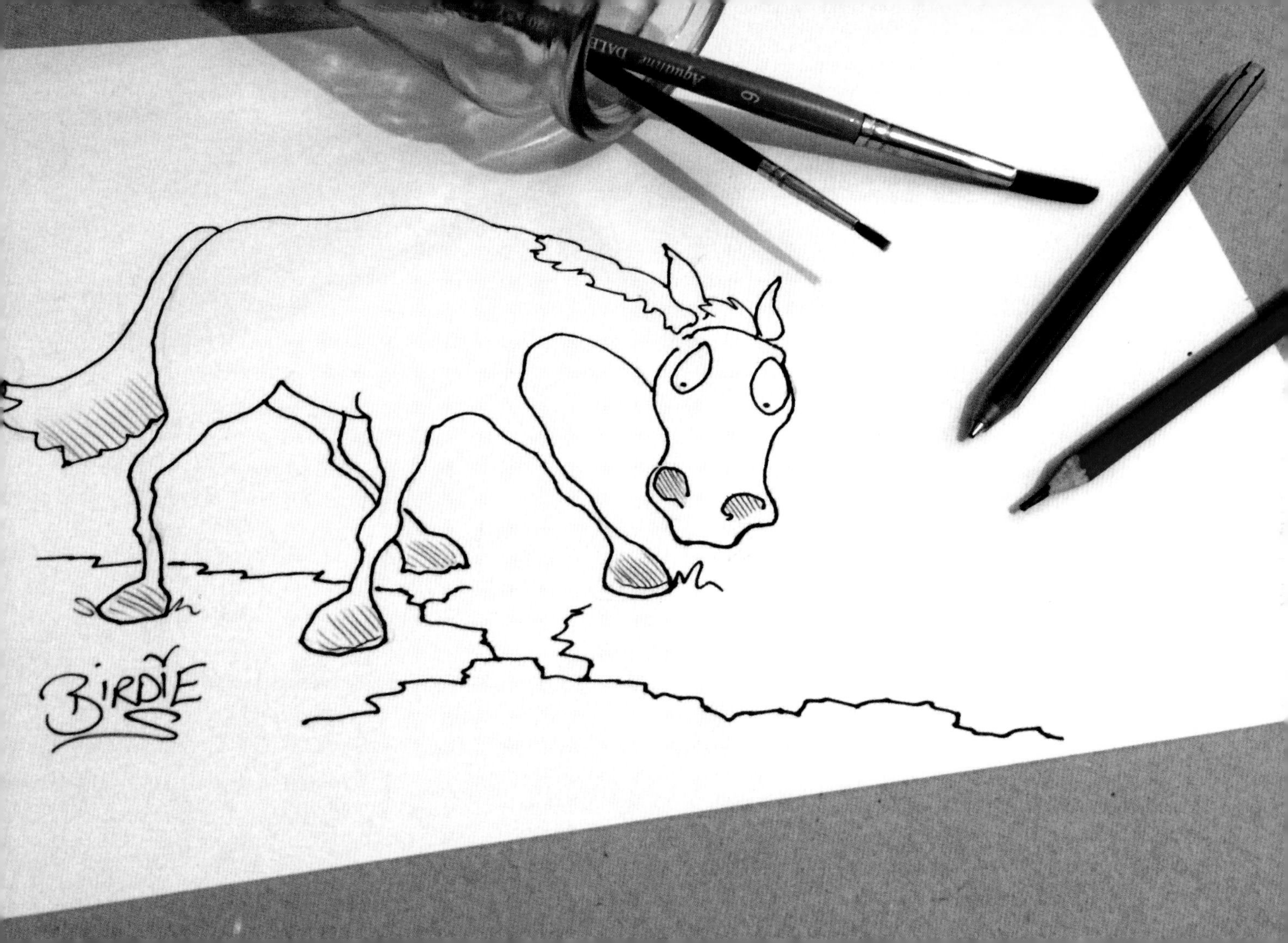
BIRDIE

THE GOOD, THE BAD AND THE BIRDIE

A bit of jockey madness on the track –
Madness were playing at Newmarket Nights

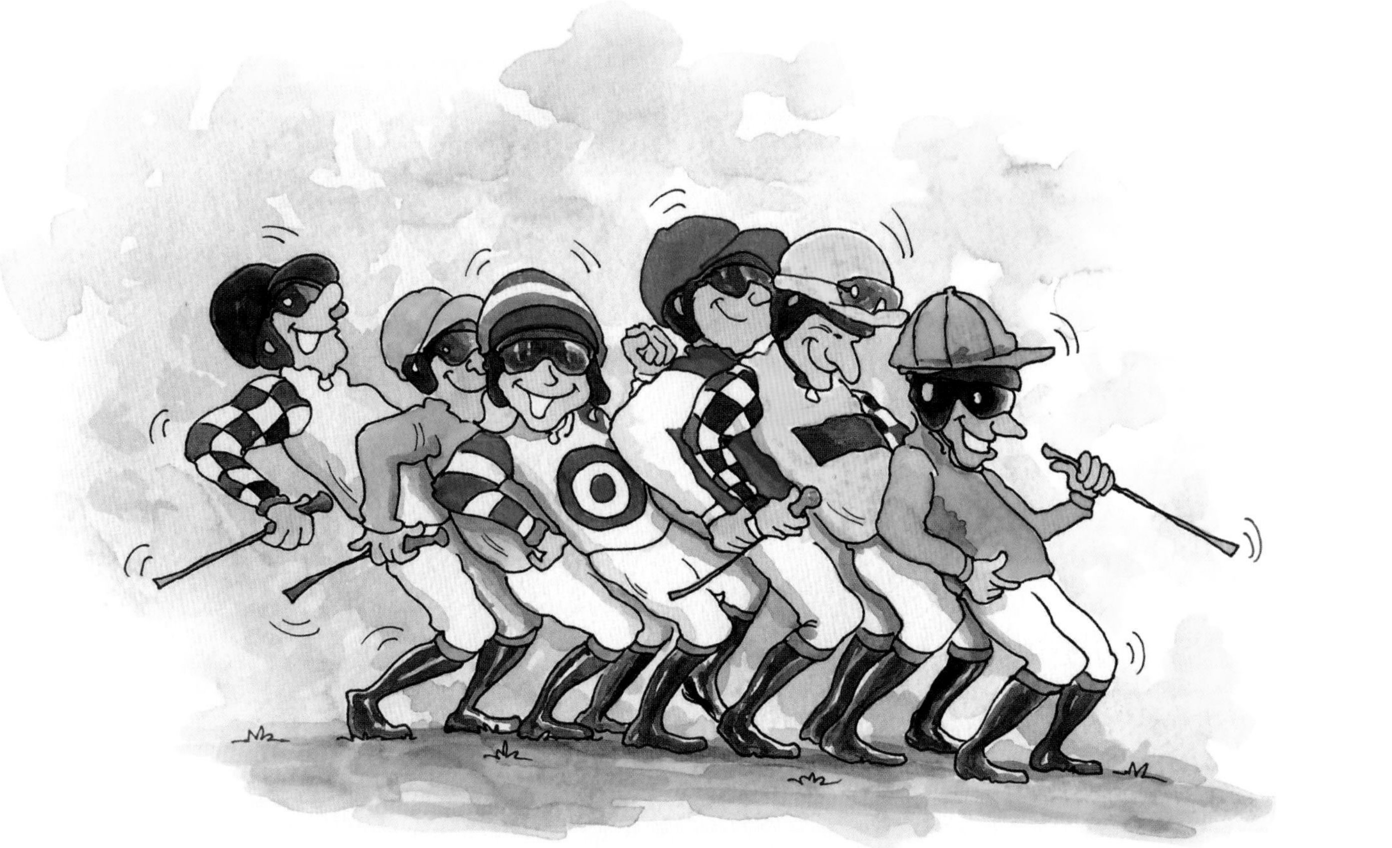

Kauto Star signs off

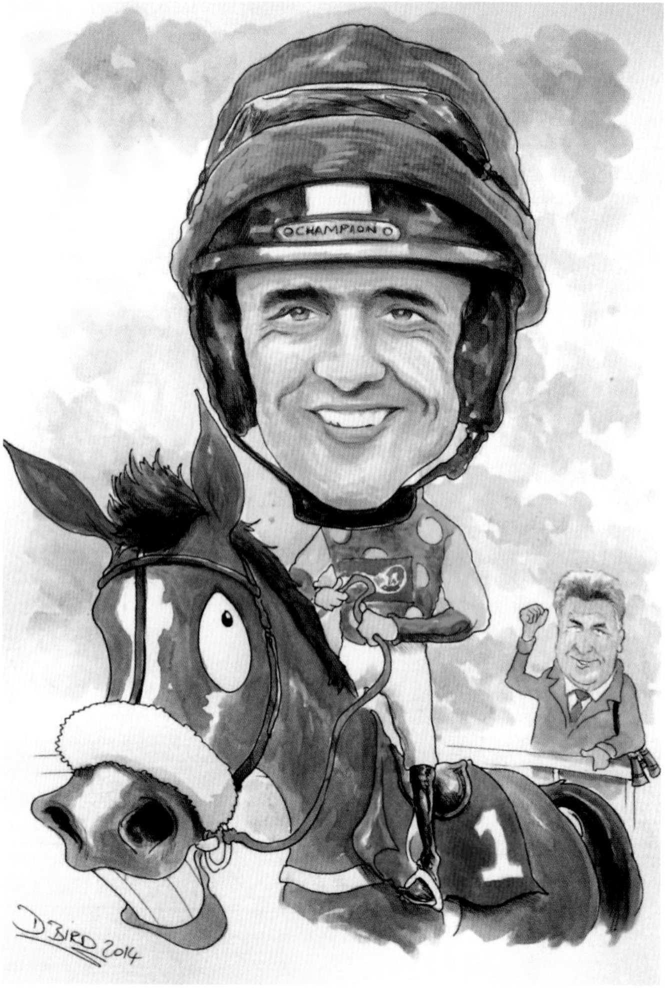
CHAMPION
1
D BIRD 2014

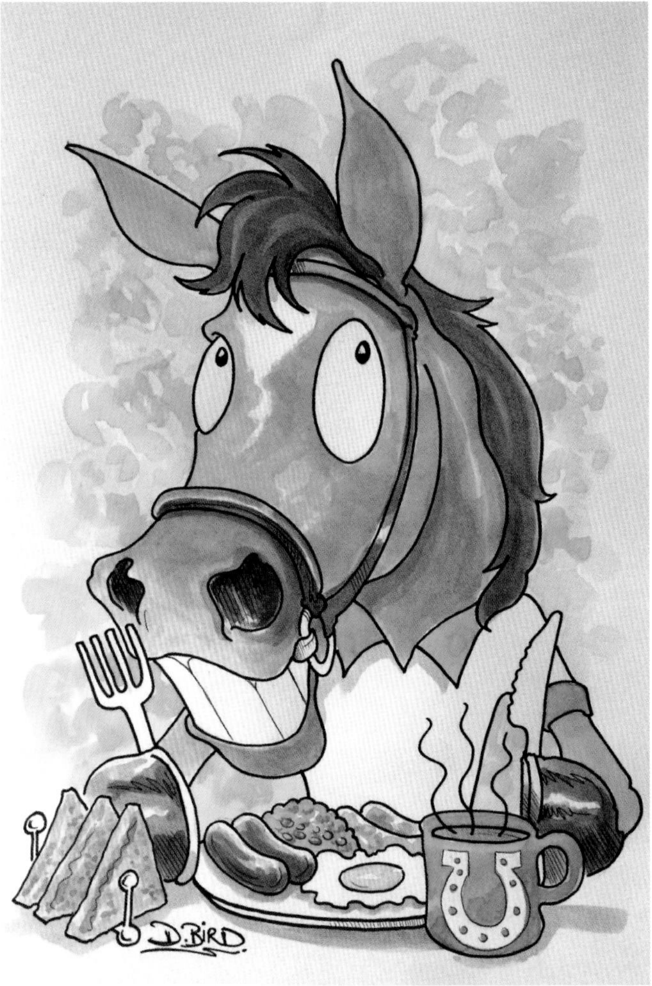
D.BIRD

A full Irish

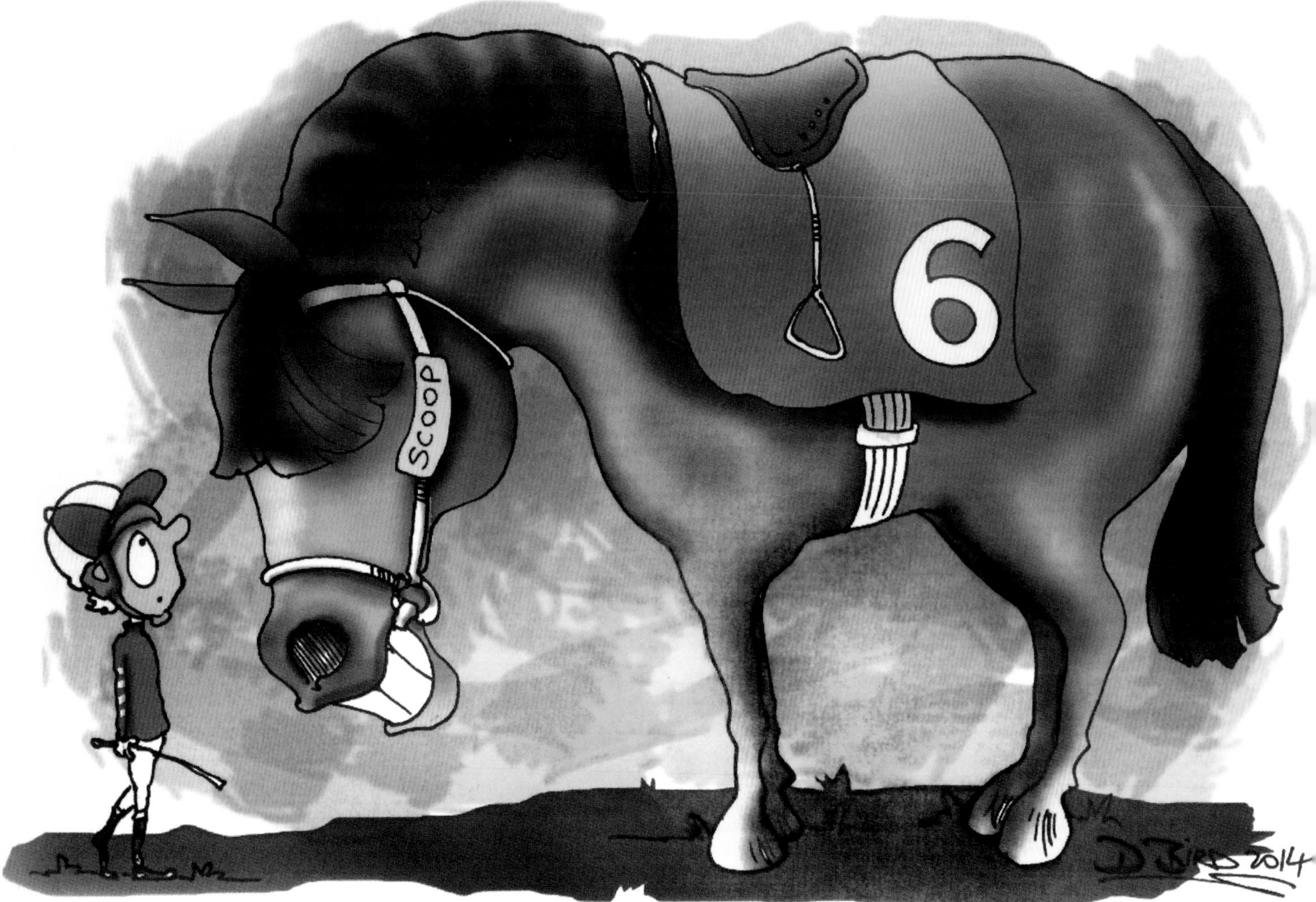
SCOOP
6
D BIRD 2014

The Scoop 6 was truly enormous

Red Cadeaux runs in the Melbourne Cup
for the fourth consecutive year

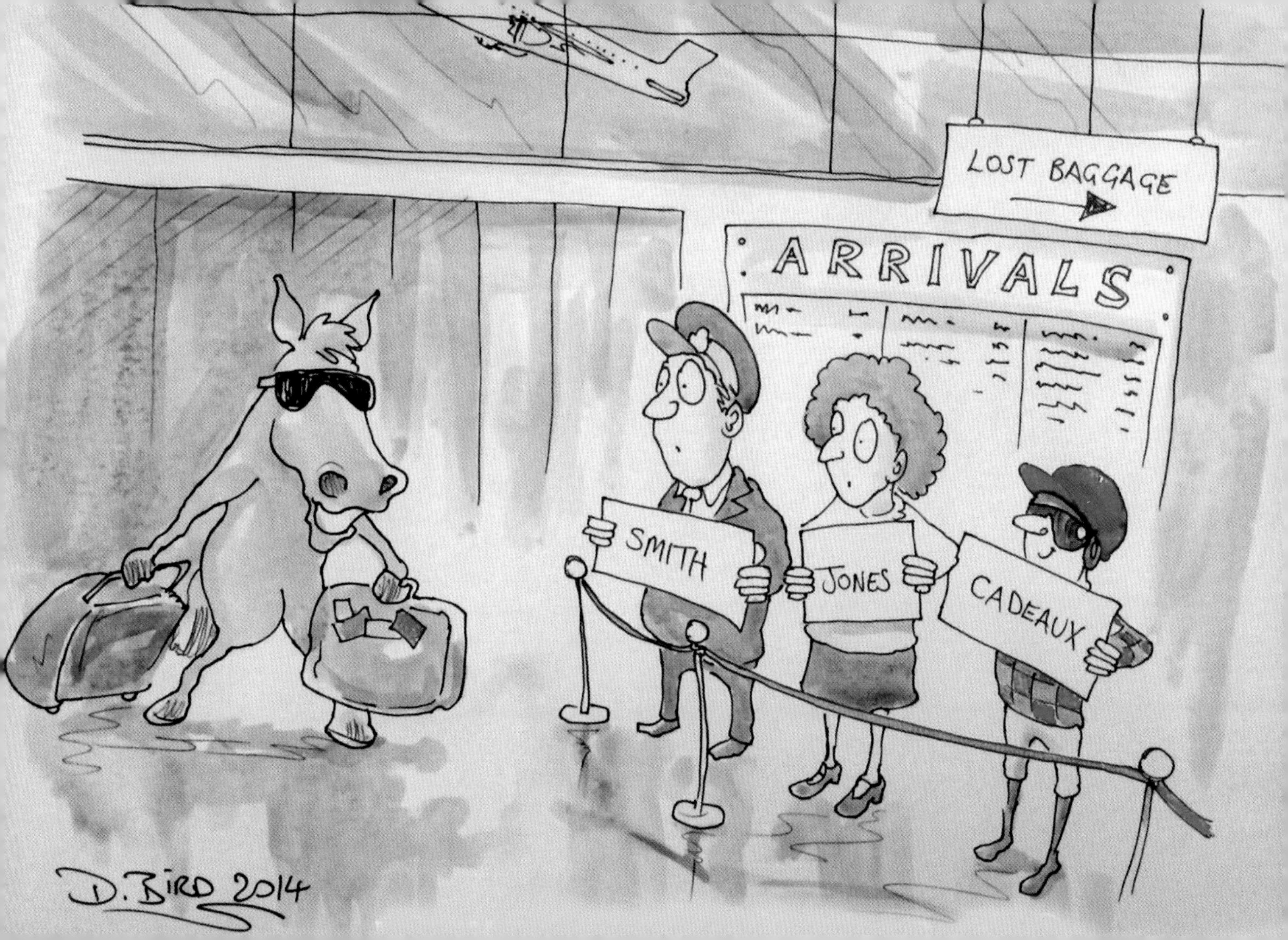
LOST BAGGAGE
ARRIVALS
SMITH
JONES
CADEAUX
D. BIRD 2014

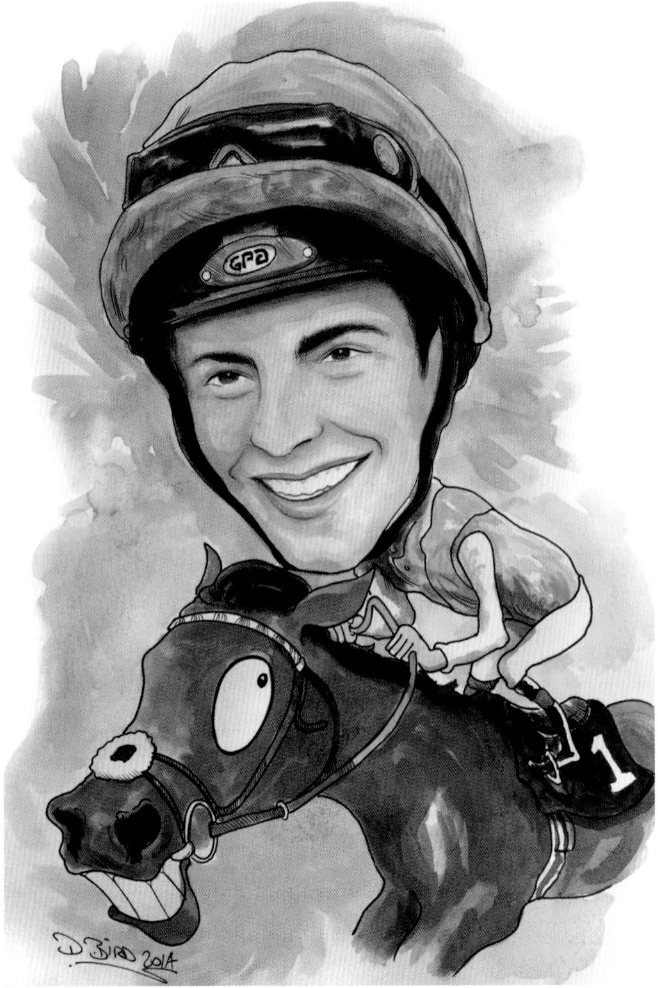
GPA
1
D. BIRD 2014

James Doyle on Kingman – stars of 2014

Katie Walsh wins in Paris
on Thousand Stars

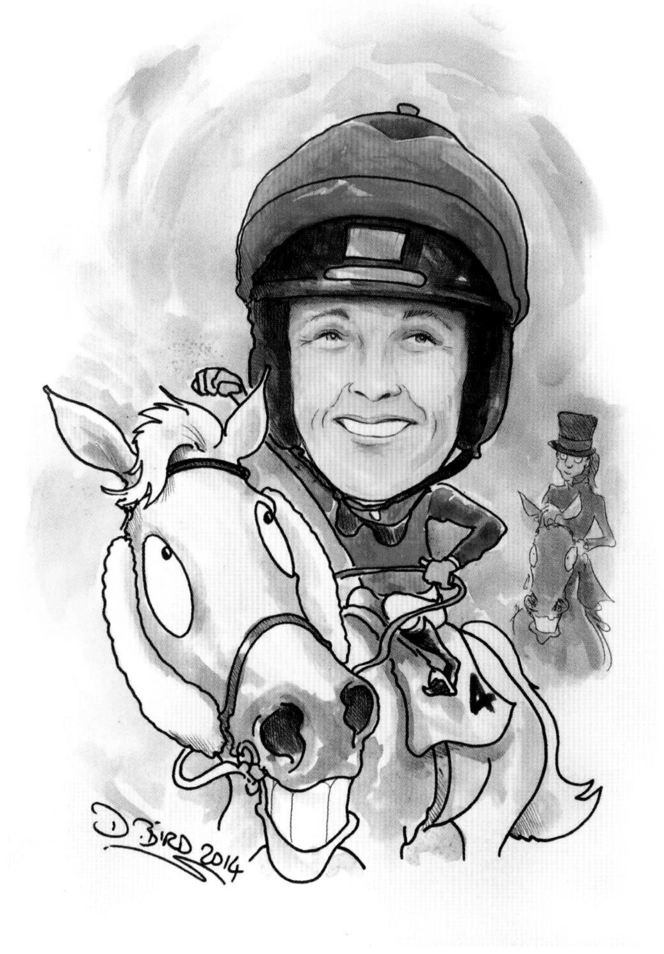
D BIRD 2014

Noble Mission follows in brother Frankel's hoofsteps

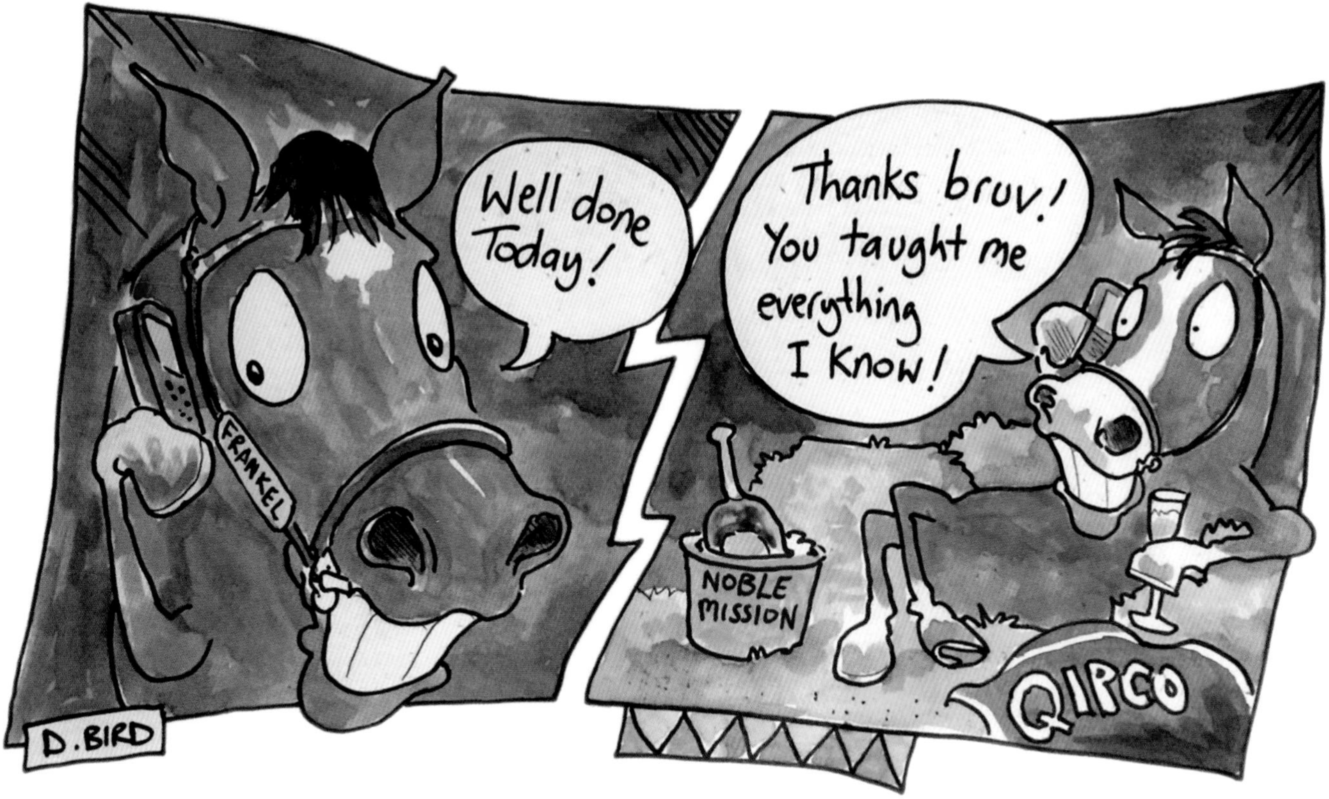
Well done Today!
Thanks bruv! You taught me everything I Know!
FRANKEL
NOBLE MISSION
QIPCO
D. BIRD

RACE 4 BRIGHTON 08/07/14
THE DAILY RACING MARKETS AT starspreads.com
3
1st 4
2:32.90*
2nd 3
3rd 1
OFFICIAL PHOTO FINISH POWERED BY
EVENT IMAGE
SIS

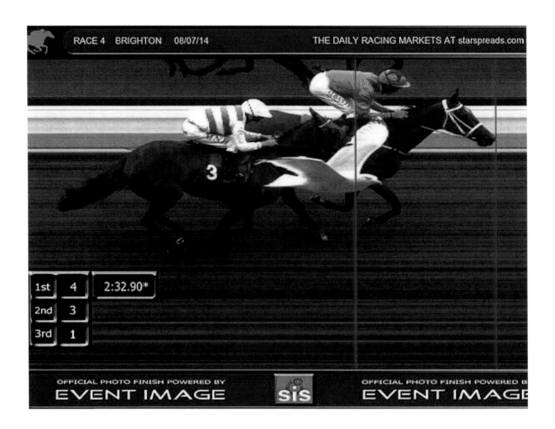

A photobombing at Brighton

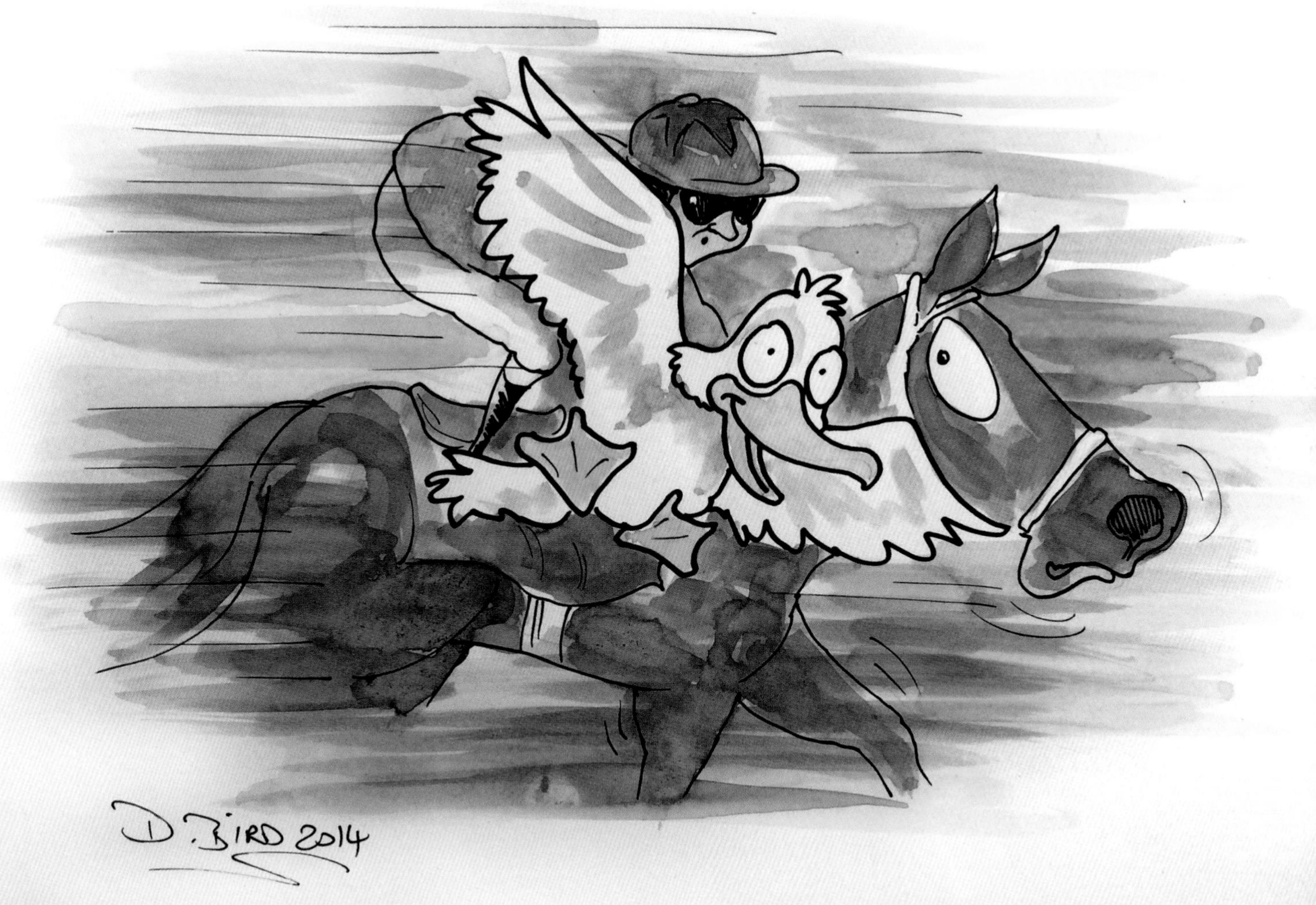
D. BIRD 2014

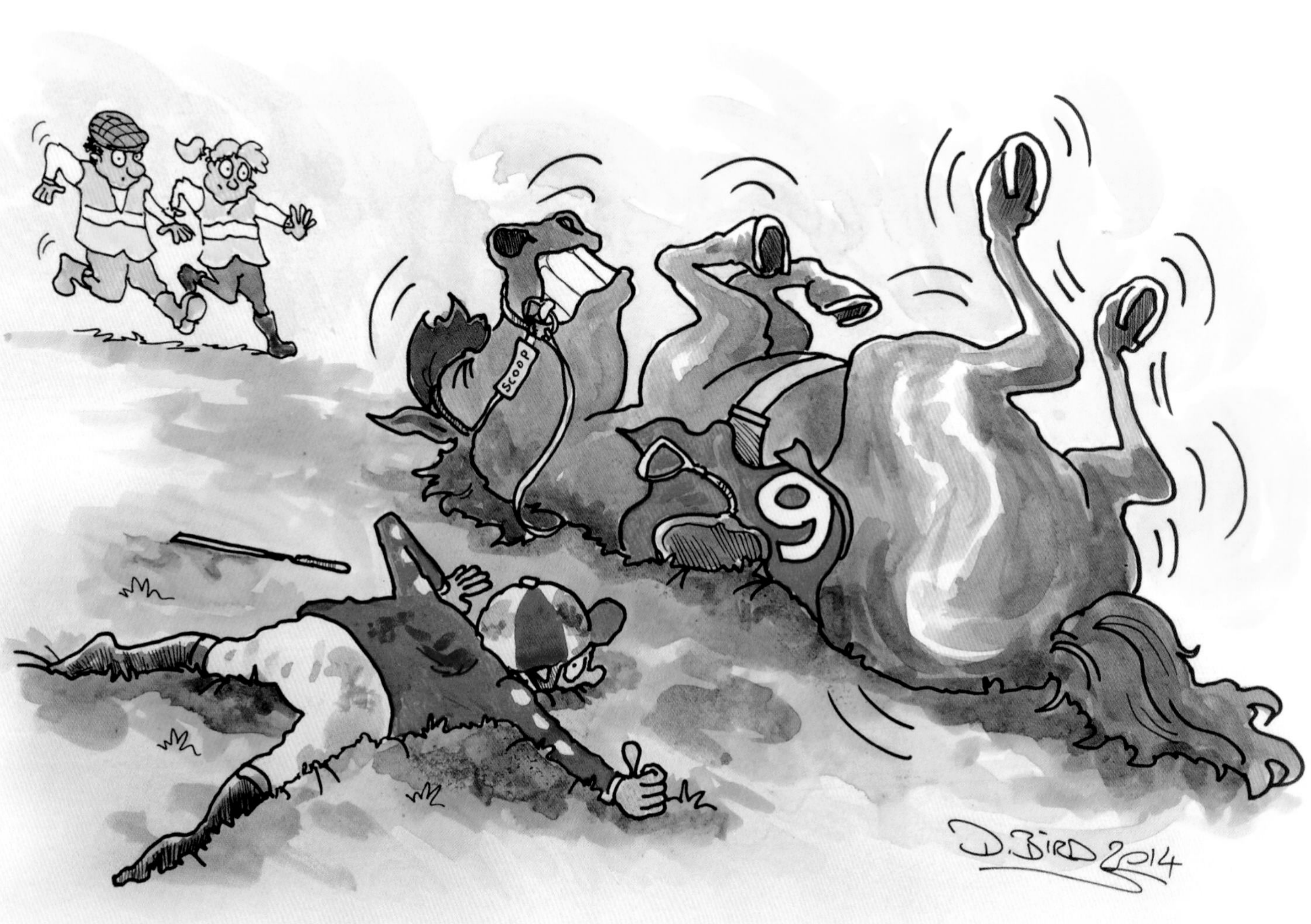
SCOOP
9
D. BIRD 2014

Scoop 6 rollover, nobody hurt … bar the punters

'Hawaiian night' at the races

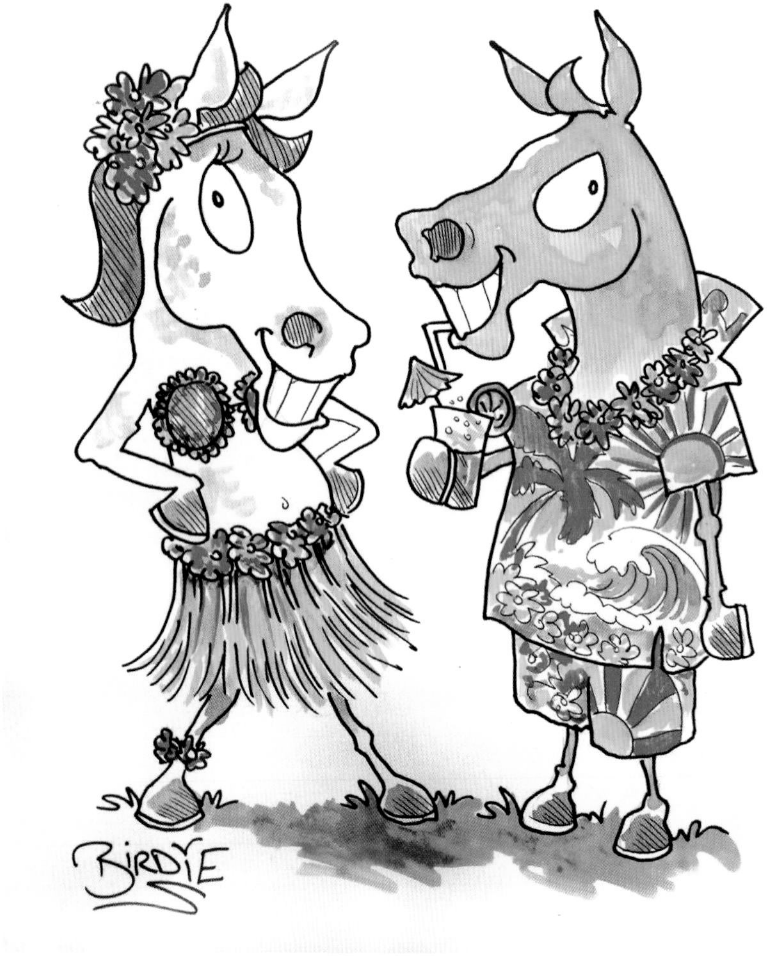
BIRDIE

Rocky Creek wins at Kempton

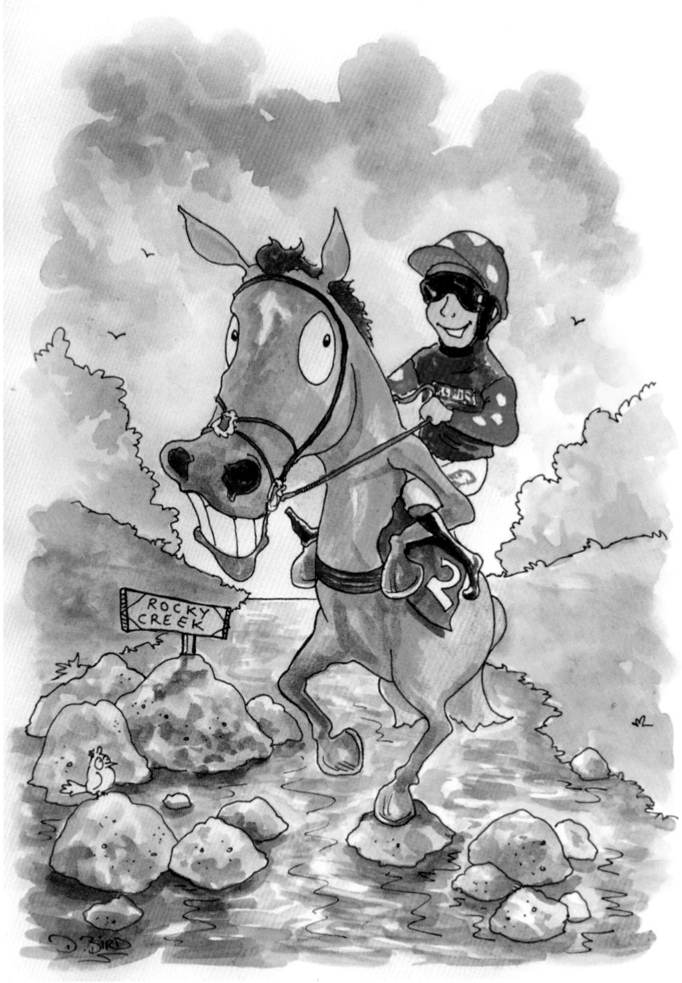
ROCKY
CREEK
2
D. BIRD

Happy in the hay

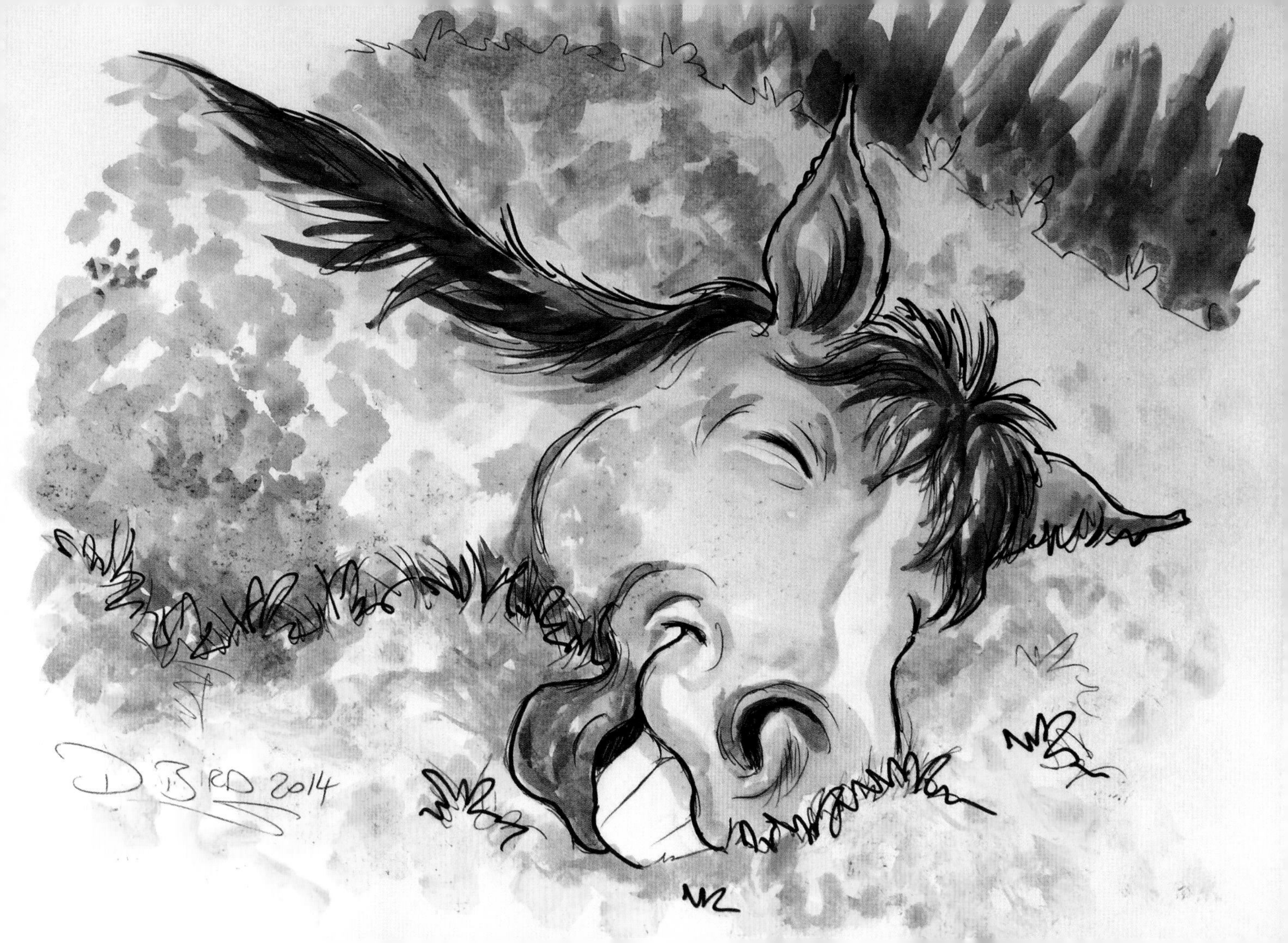
D. BIRD 2014

Chris Hayes and Panama Hat complete a four timer in Ireland

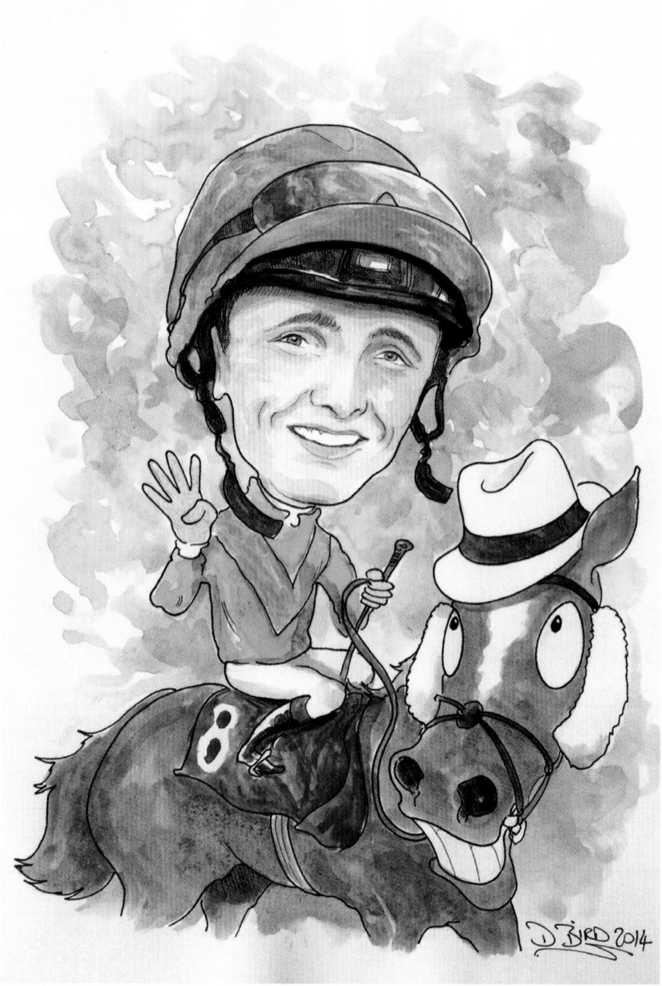
8
D BYRD 2014

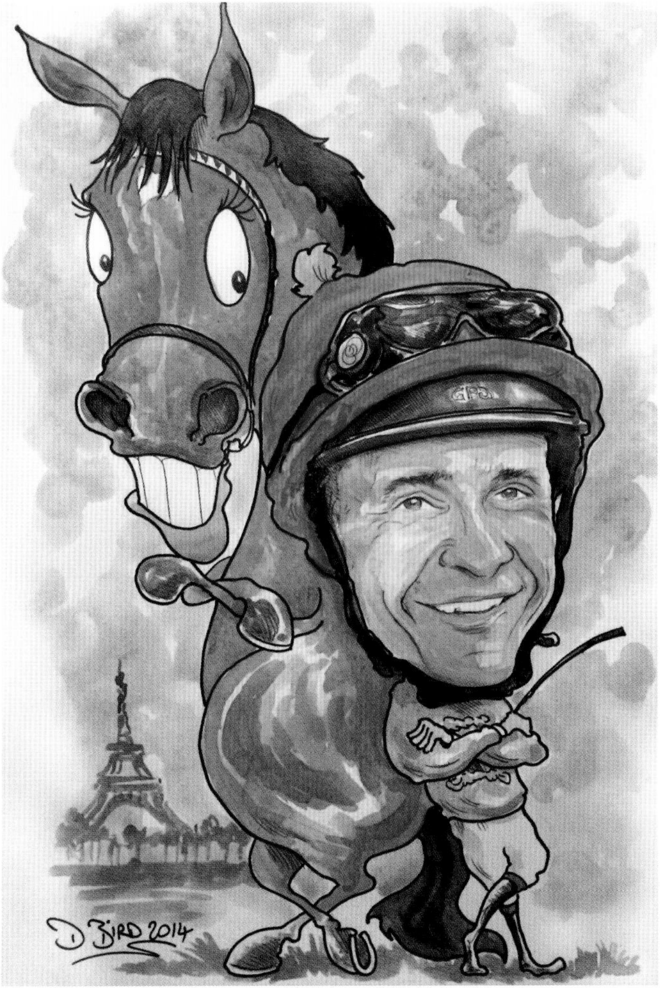
D BIRD 2014

Treve and Thierry Jarnet have back to back wins in the Arc

The Poppy Day centenary

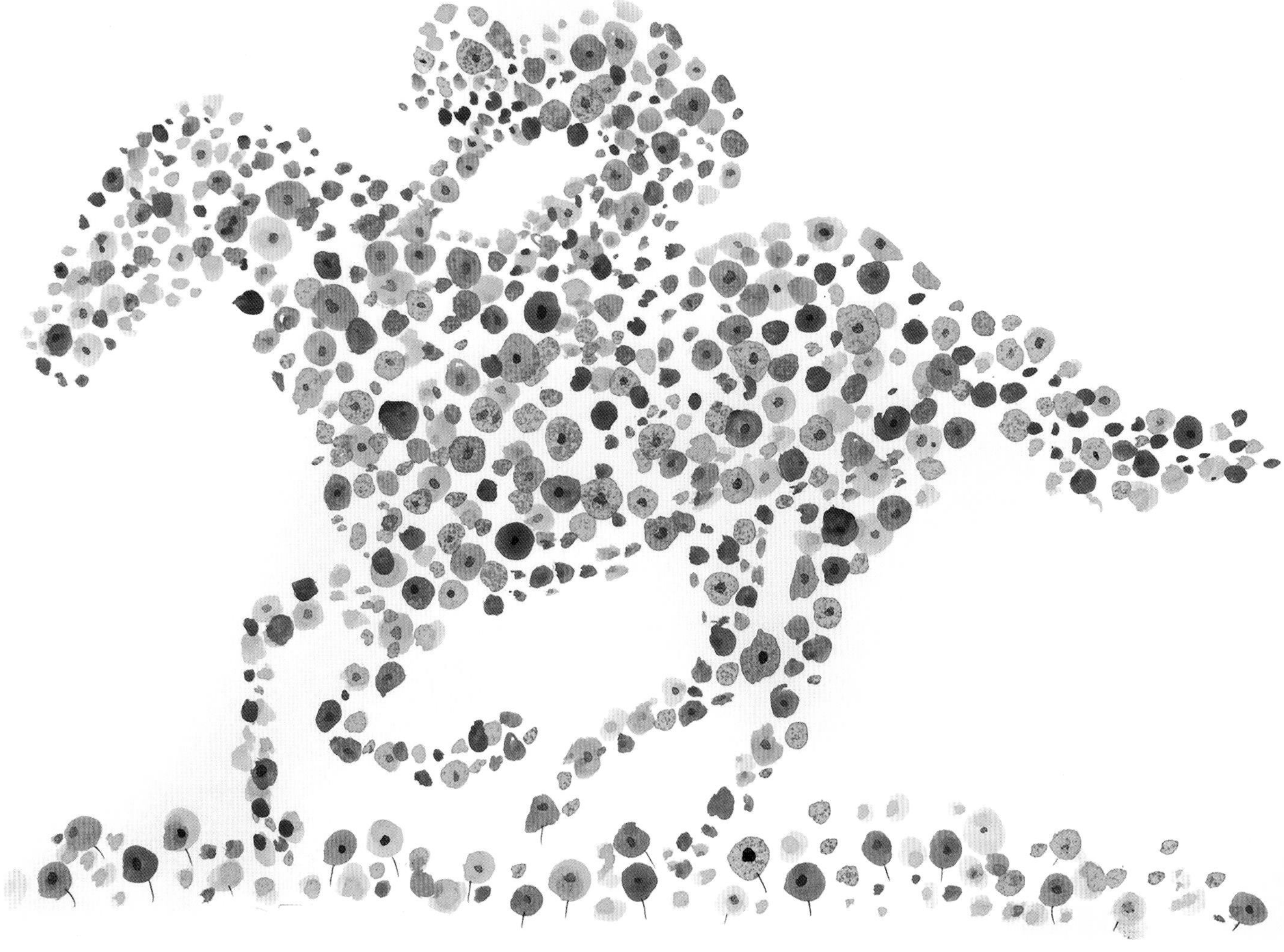

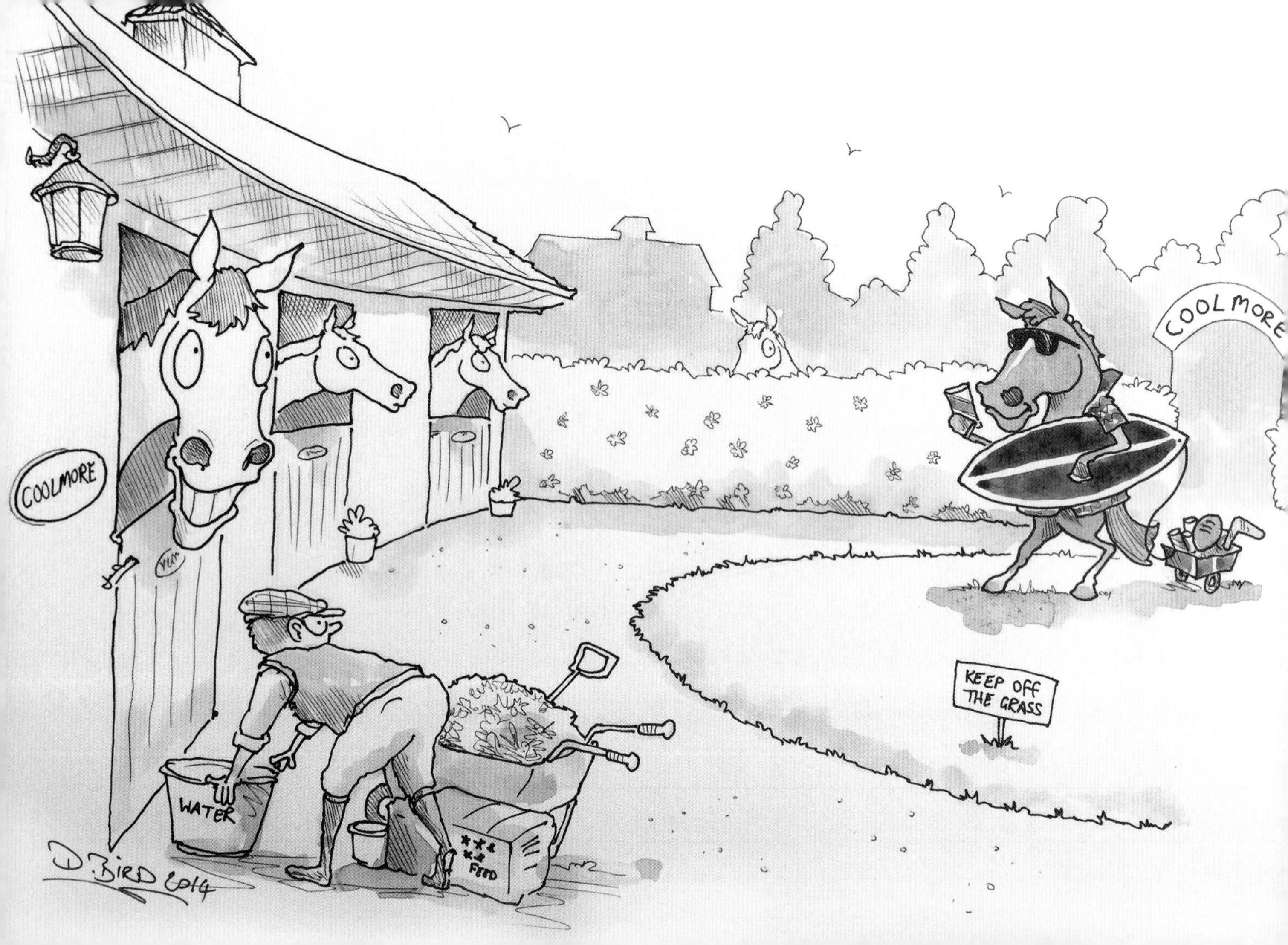
COOLMORE
COOLMORE
YUM
WATER
FEED
KEEP OFF THE GRASS
D. BIRD 2014

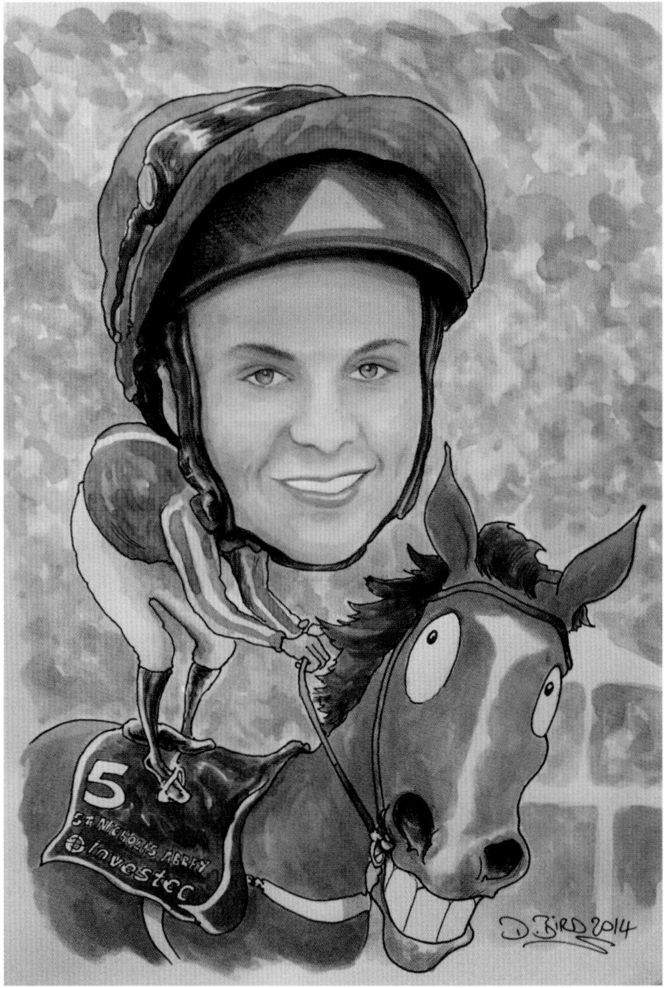
5
ST NICHOLAS ABBEY
Investec
D. BIRD 2014

RIP St Nicholas Abbey – Joseph O'Brien's Breeders Cup and dual Coronation Cup winner dies in January 2014

Opposite: Derby winner Australia retires to stud

‘Mummy, I want a balloon like that’ –
Laytown is the last beach racecourse in Ireland

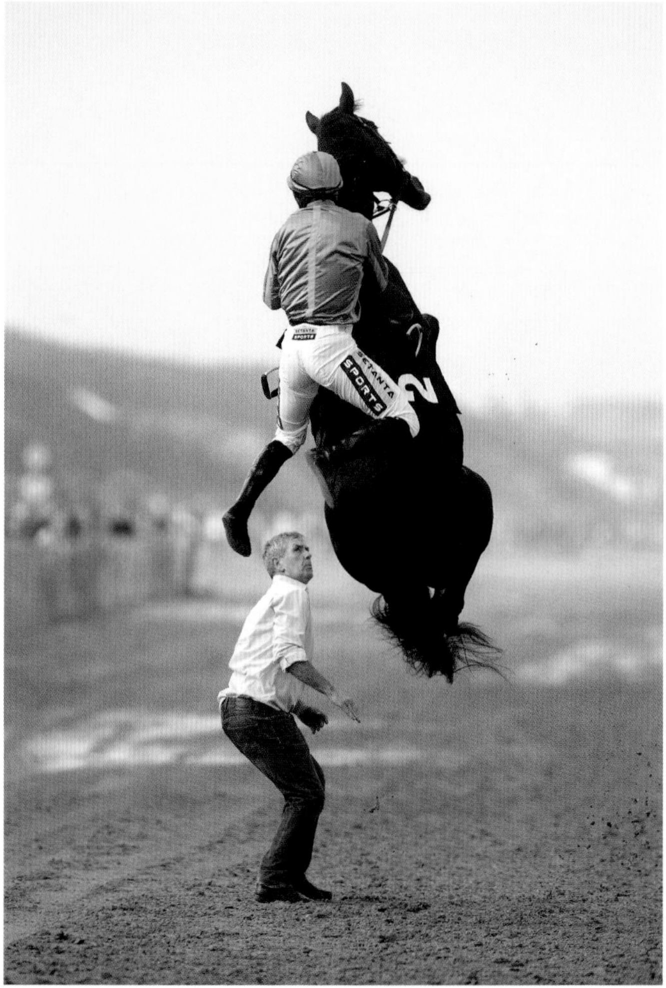
SETANTA SPORTS

© Pat Healy

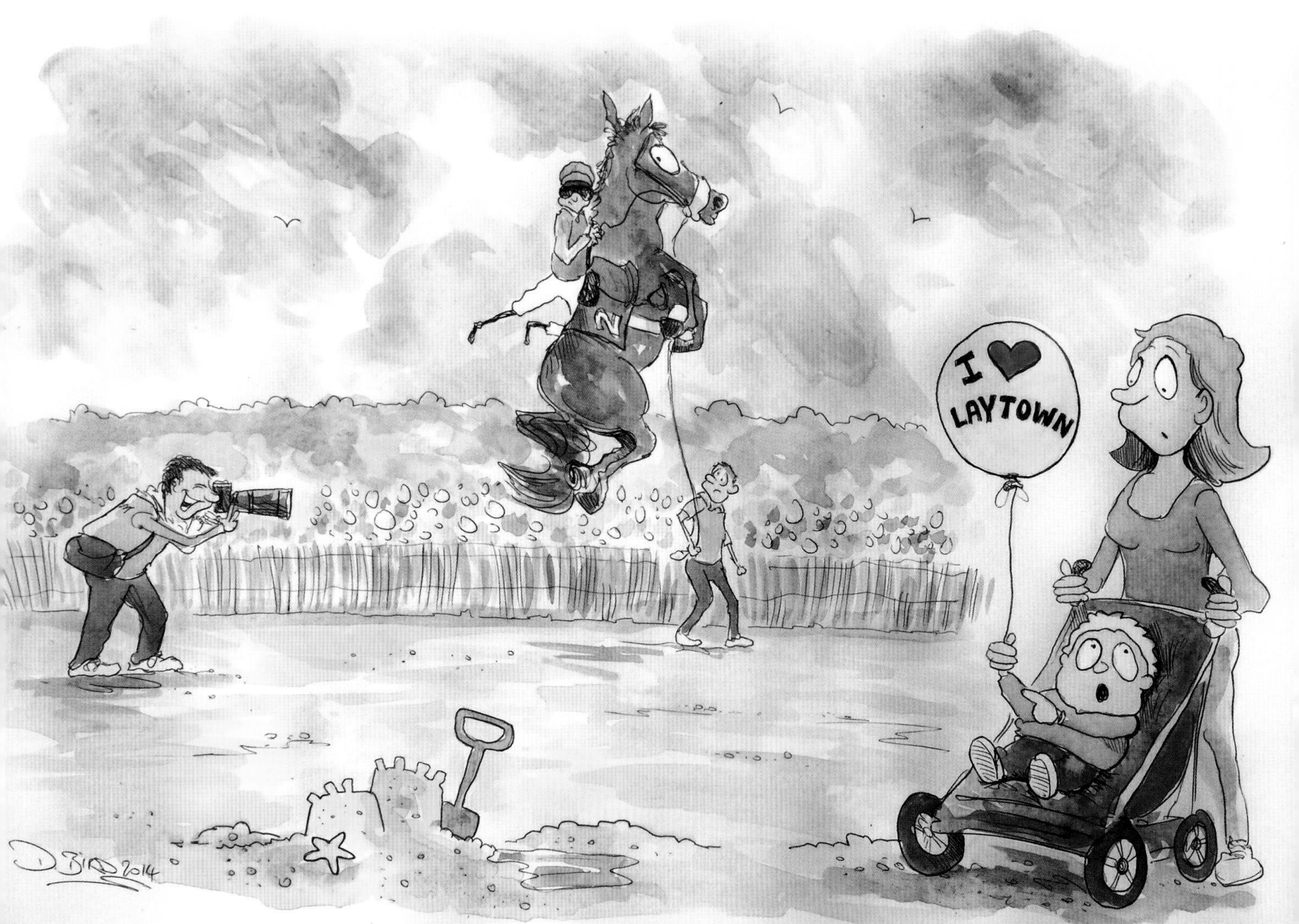

I ♥ LAYTOWN
D. BIRD 2014

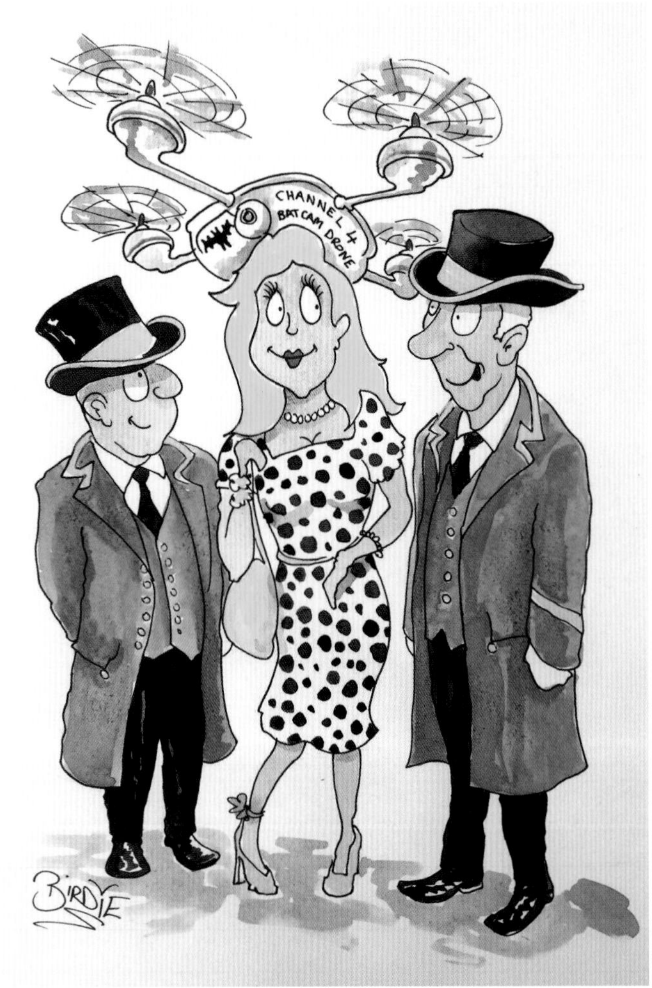
CHANNEL 4
BAT CAM DRONE
BIRDIE

Channel 4 introduce drones
to their Royal Ascot coverage

Sam Twiston-Davies and
The New One – five times
winners at Cheltenham

British hope Telescope searches for victory
in the Breeders' Cup at Santa Anita

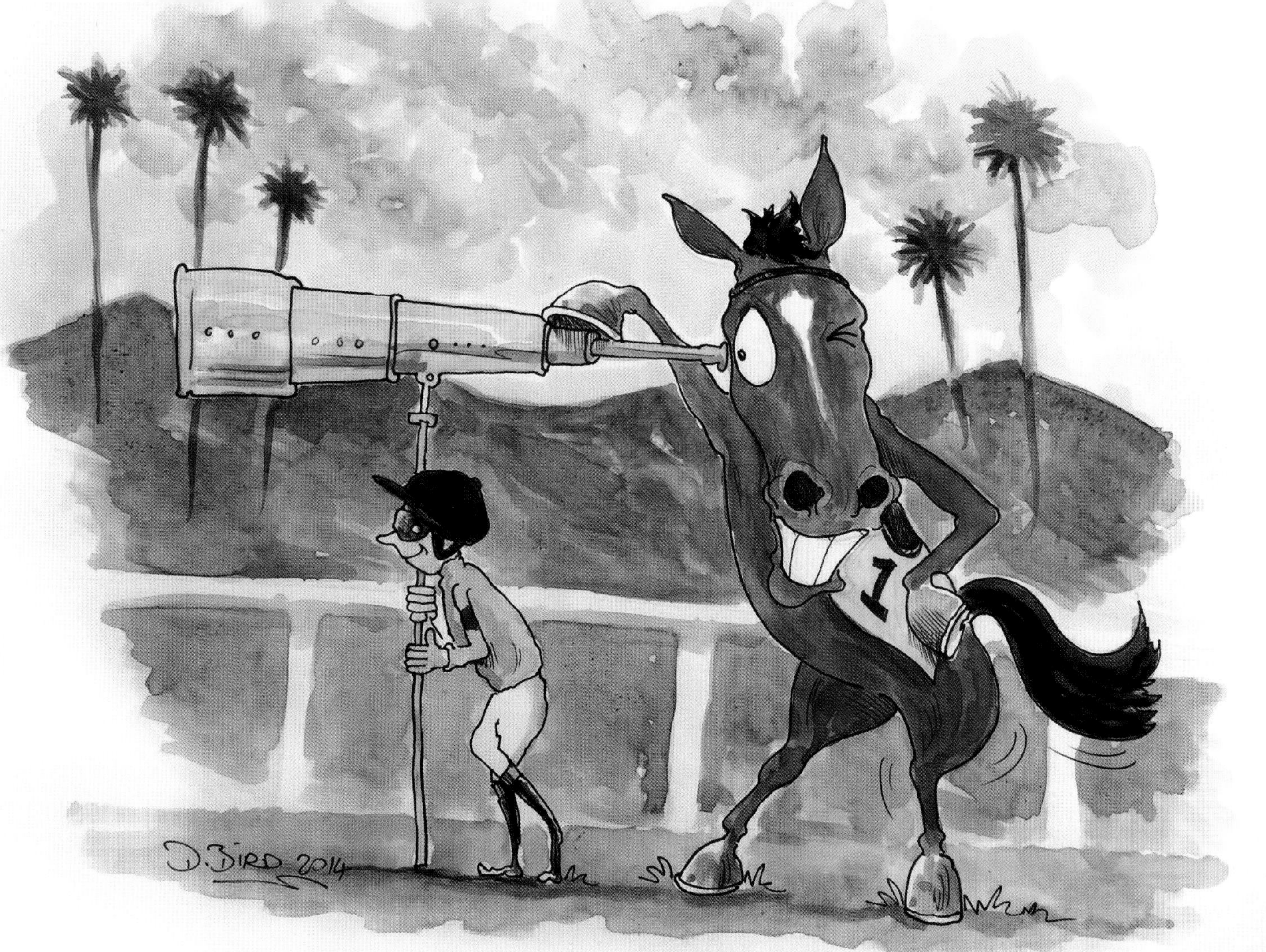
1
D.BIRD 2014

Thumbs up to Top Notch
Tonto as he wins at York

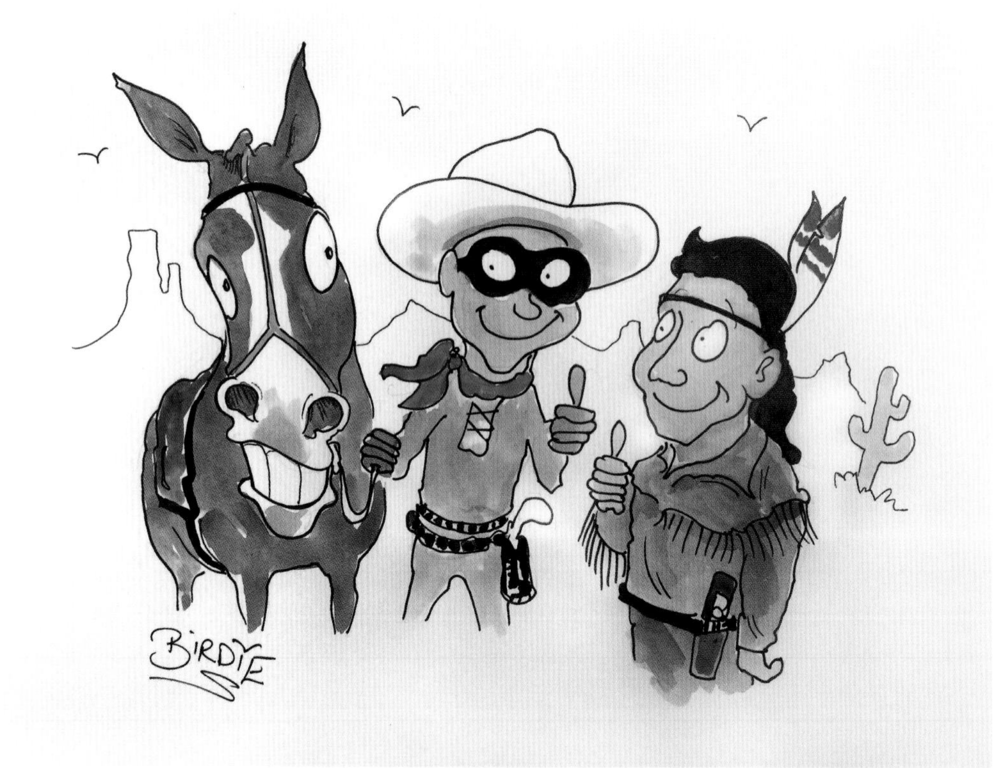
BIRDIE

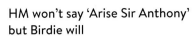

HM won't say 'Arise Sir Anthony'
but Birdie will

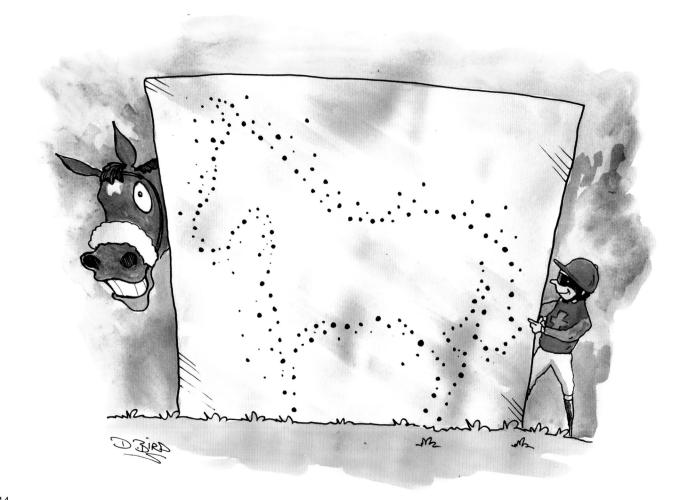

'No Philip. It's June. They are not in season.'

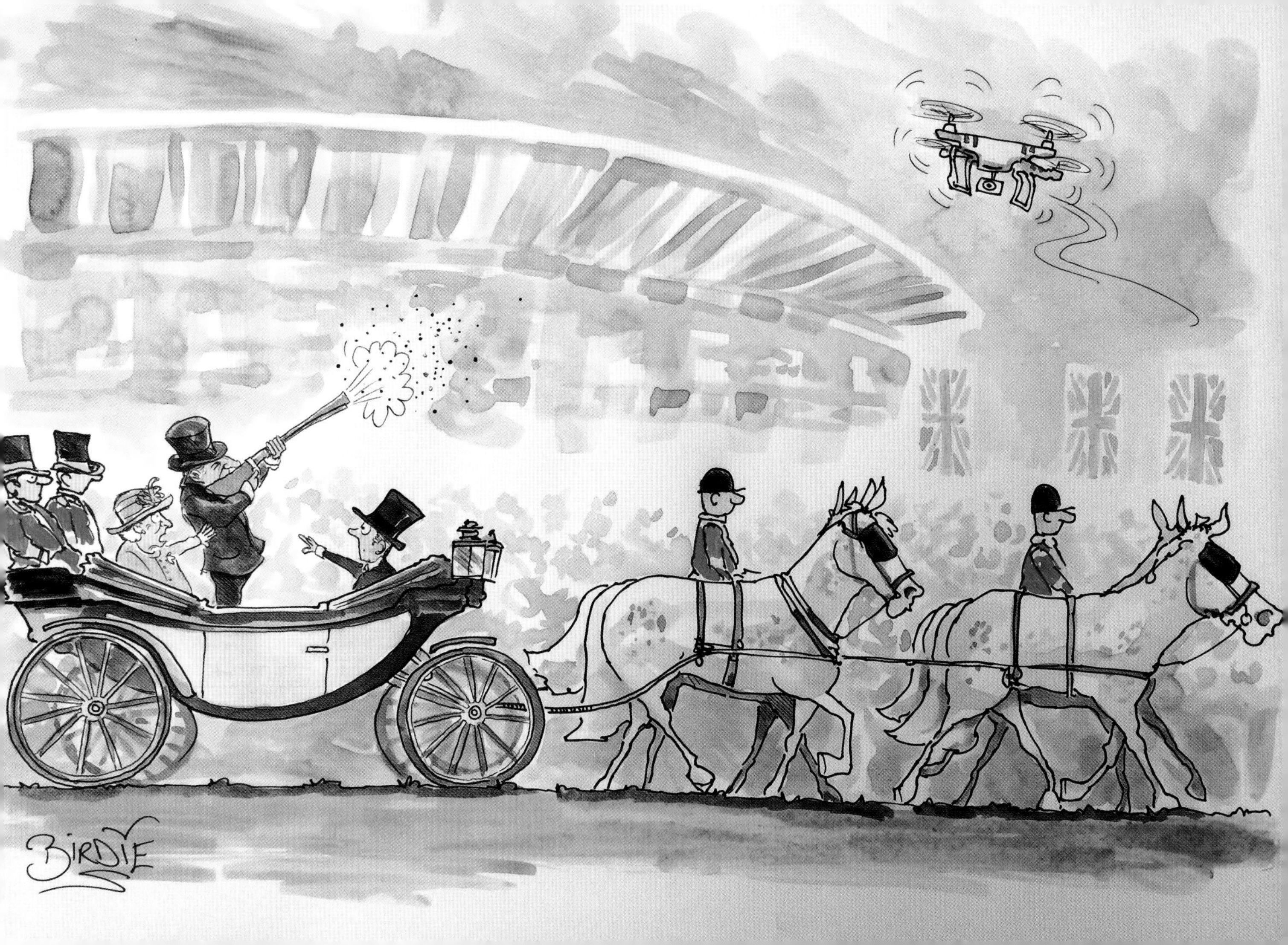
BIRDIE

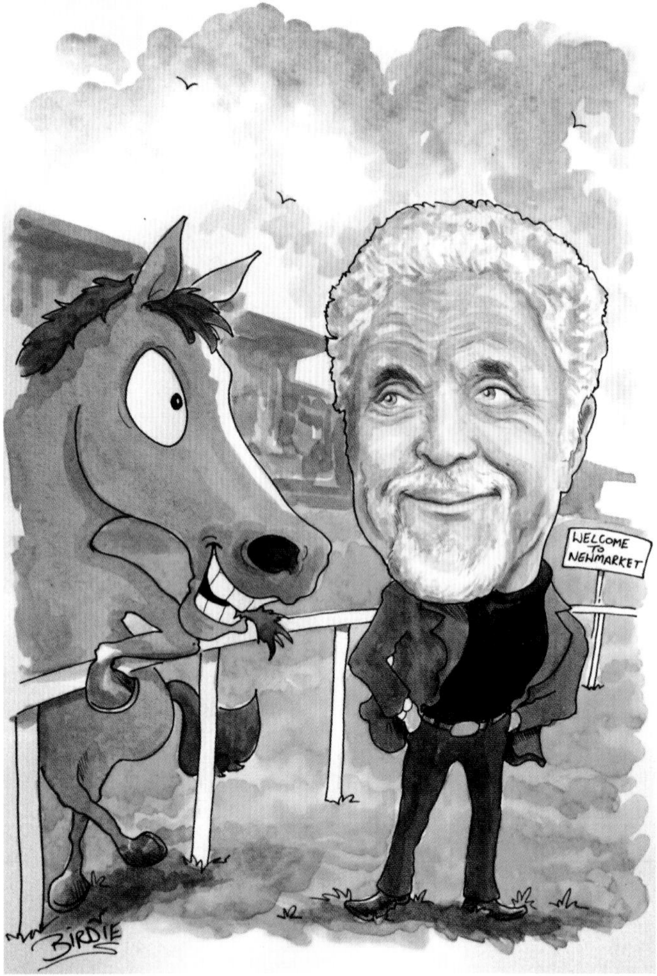
WELCOME TO NEWMARKET
BIRDIE

Tom Jones joins the Newmarket Nights

Hollywood star Bo Derek gives 10 out of 10 to British runner Toast Of New York

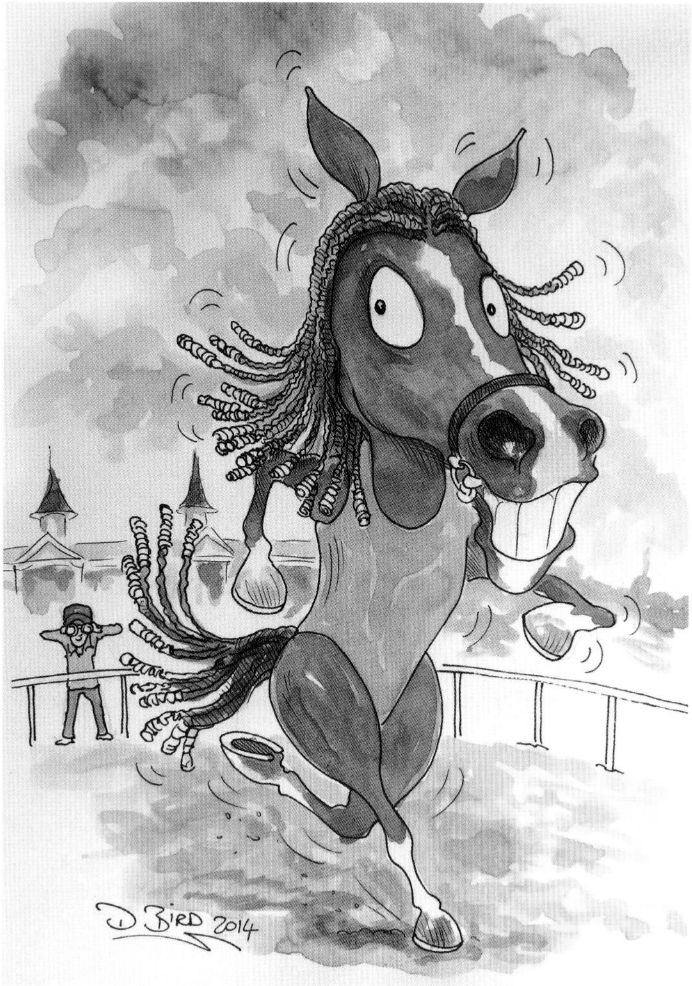
D BIRD 2014

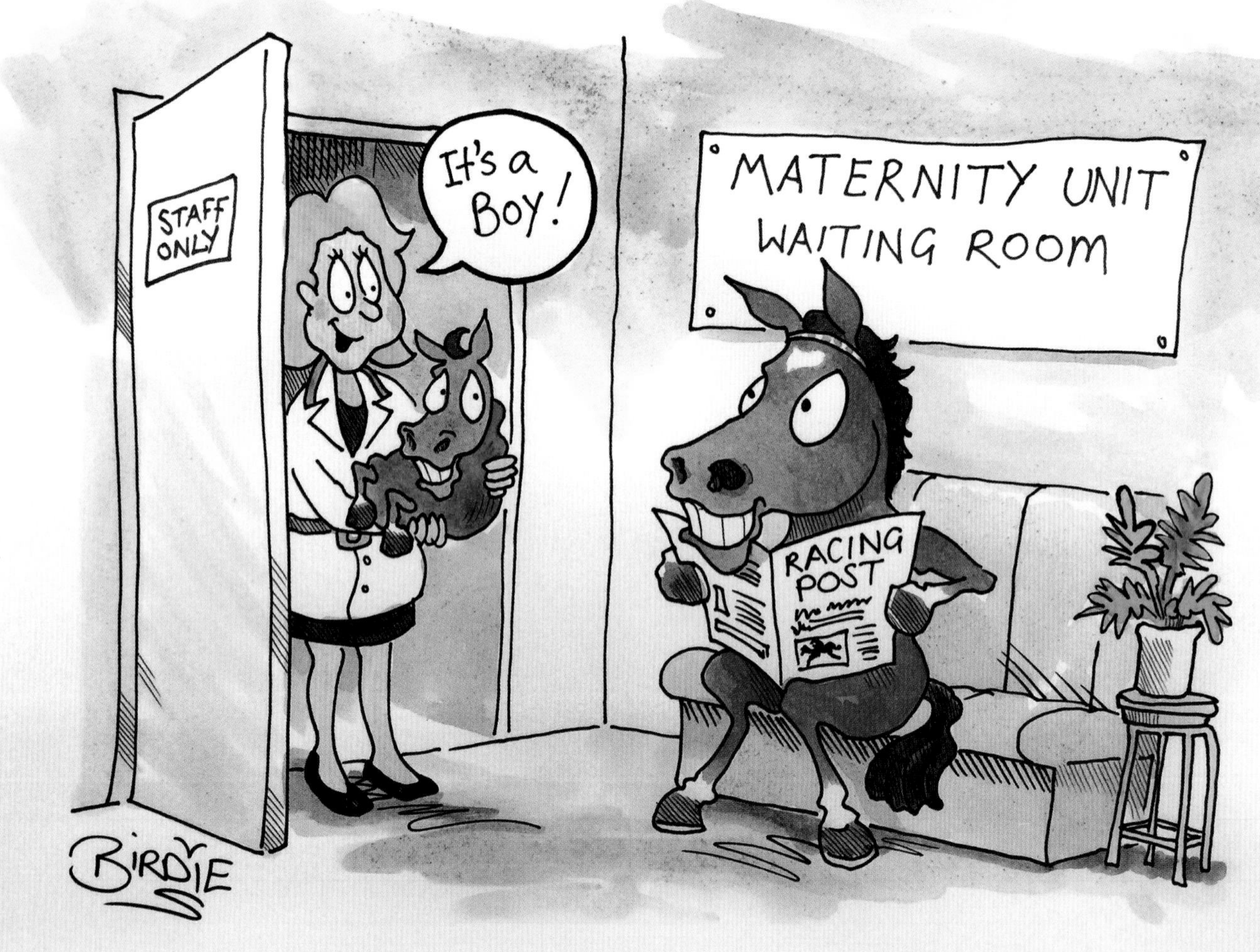
STAFF ONLY
It's a Boy!
MATERNITY UNIT
WAITING ROOM
RACING POST
BIRDIE

Australian wonder mare Black Caviar has her first foal – a filly

Opposite: Frankel's first foal is born, January 2014

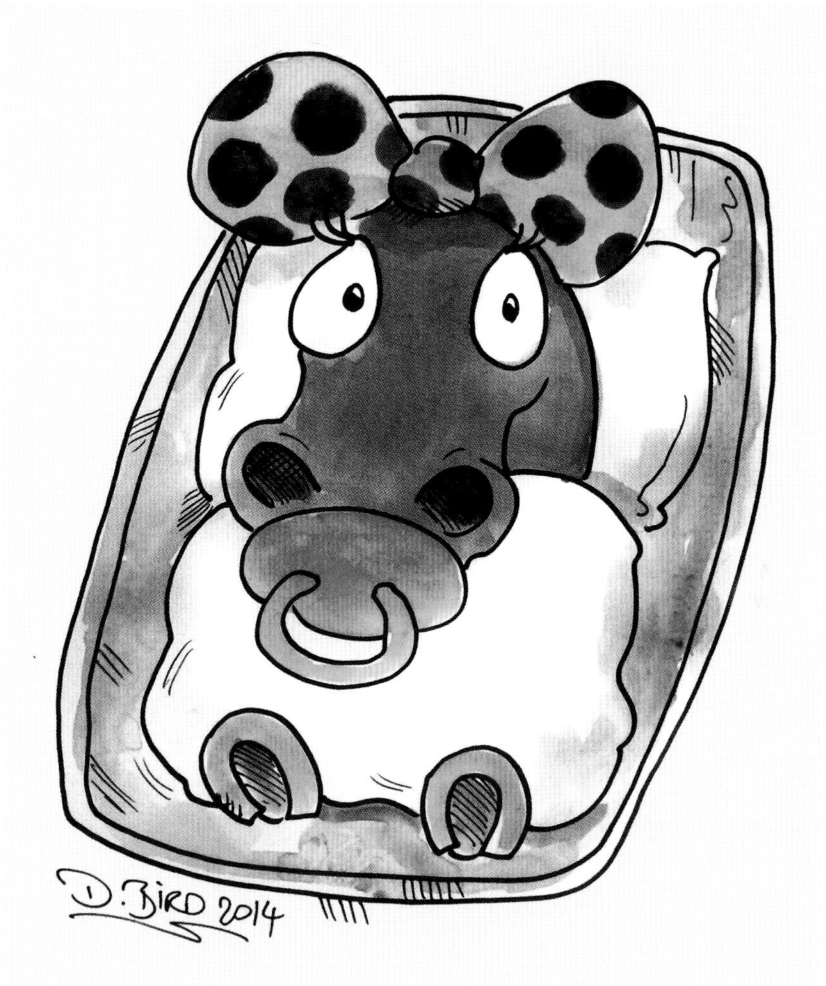
D. BIRD 2014

African Story wins the Dubai World Cup

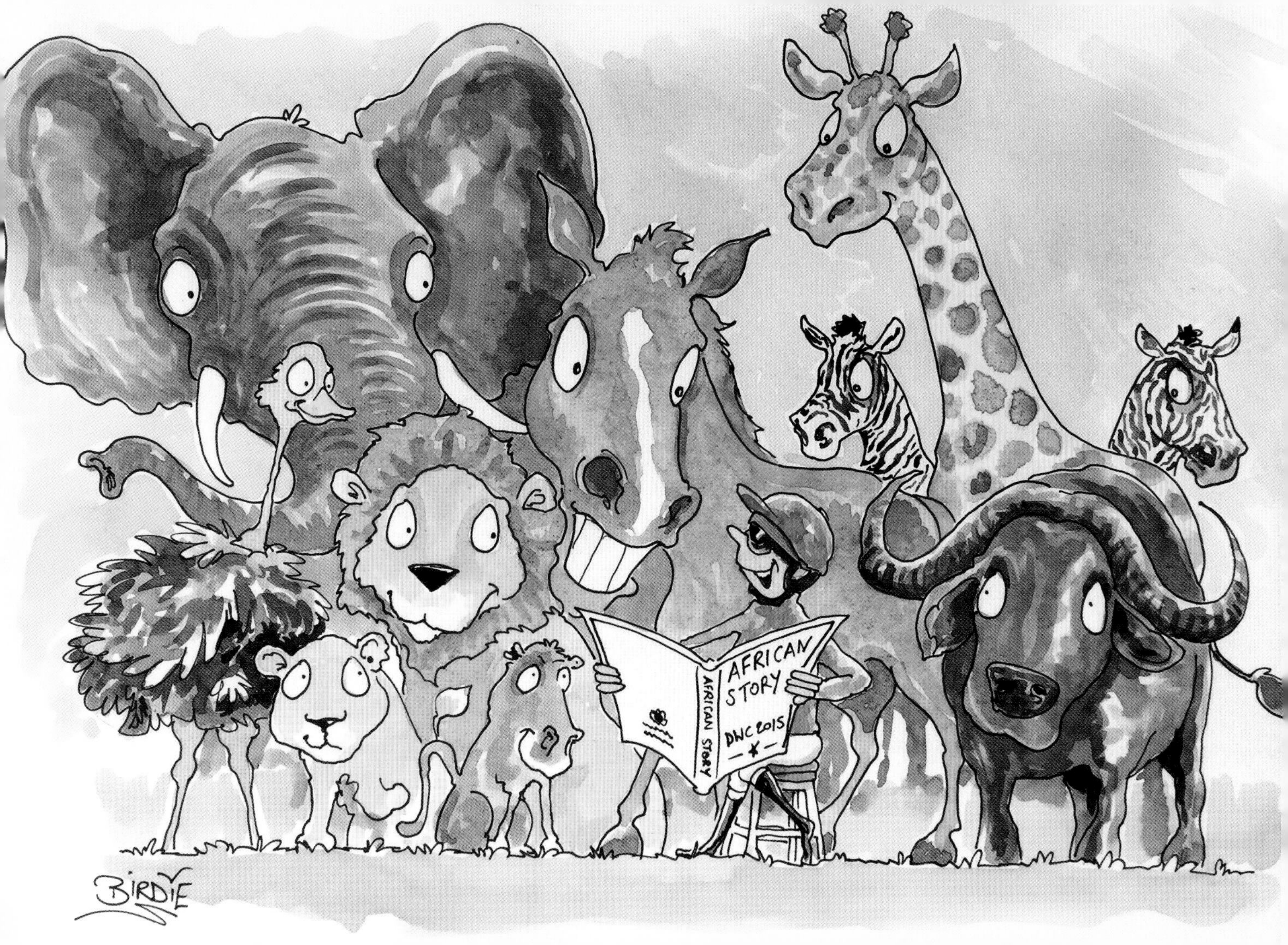
AFRICAN STORY
DNC 2015
AFRICAN STORY
BIRDIE

Ryan Moore wins the Japan
Cup on Gentildonna

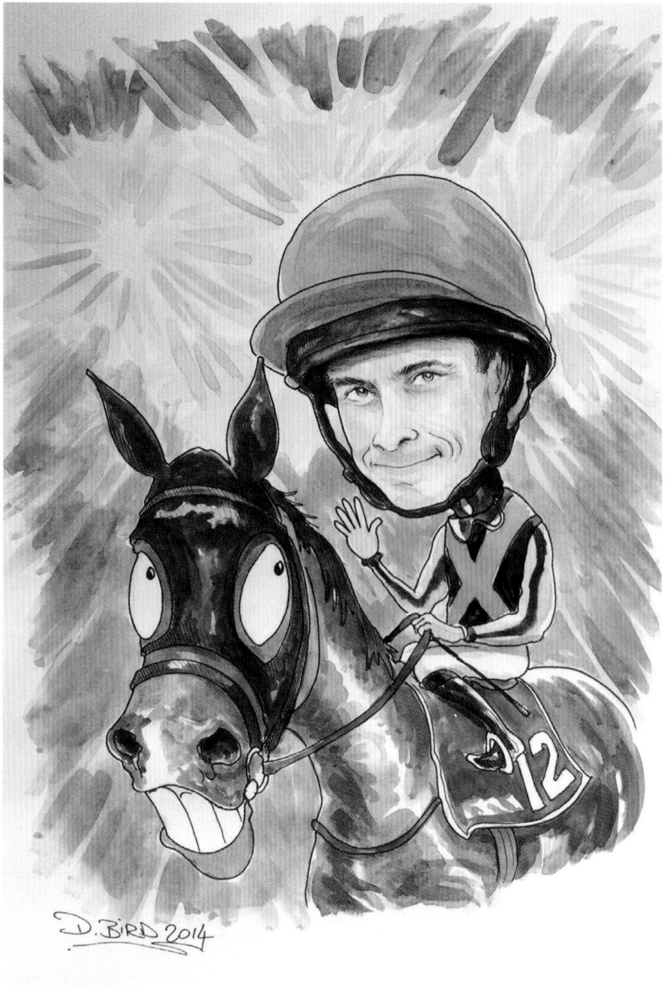
12
D. BIRD 2014

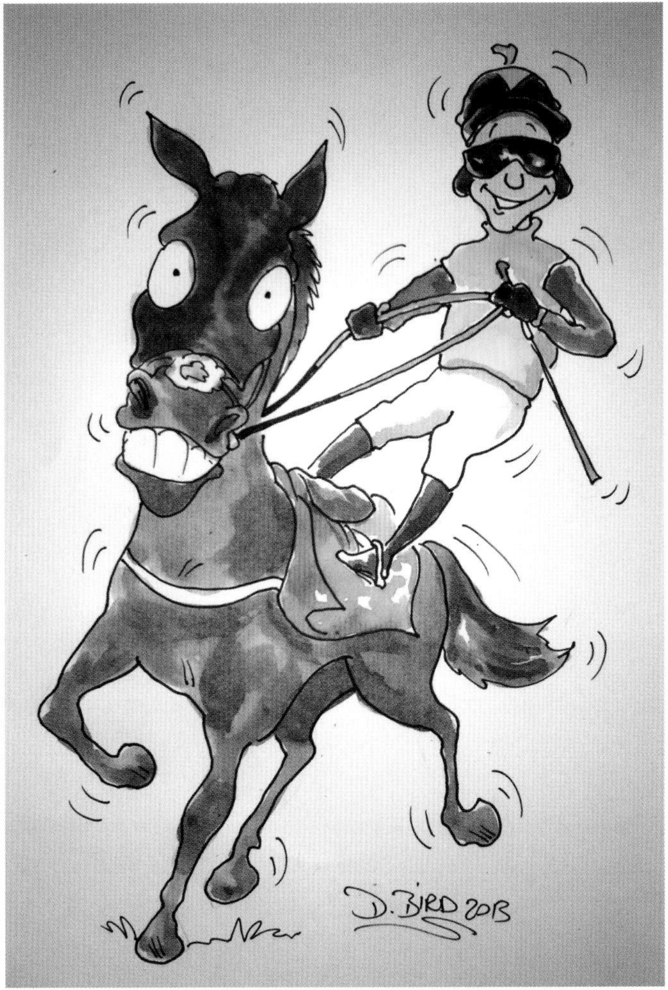
D. BIRD 2013

Deep Trouble – Leighton Aspell somehow stays aboard him to win at Sandown

'Who do you think you are? Aidan O'Brien?'

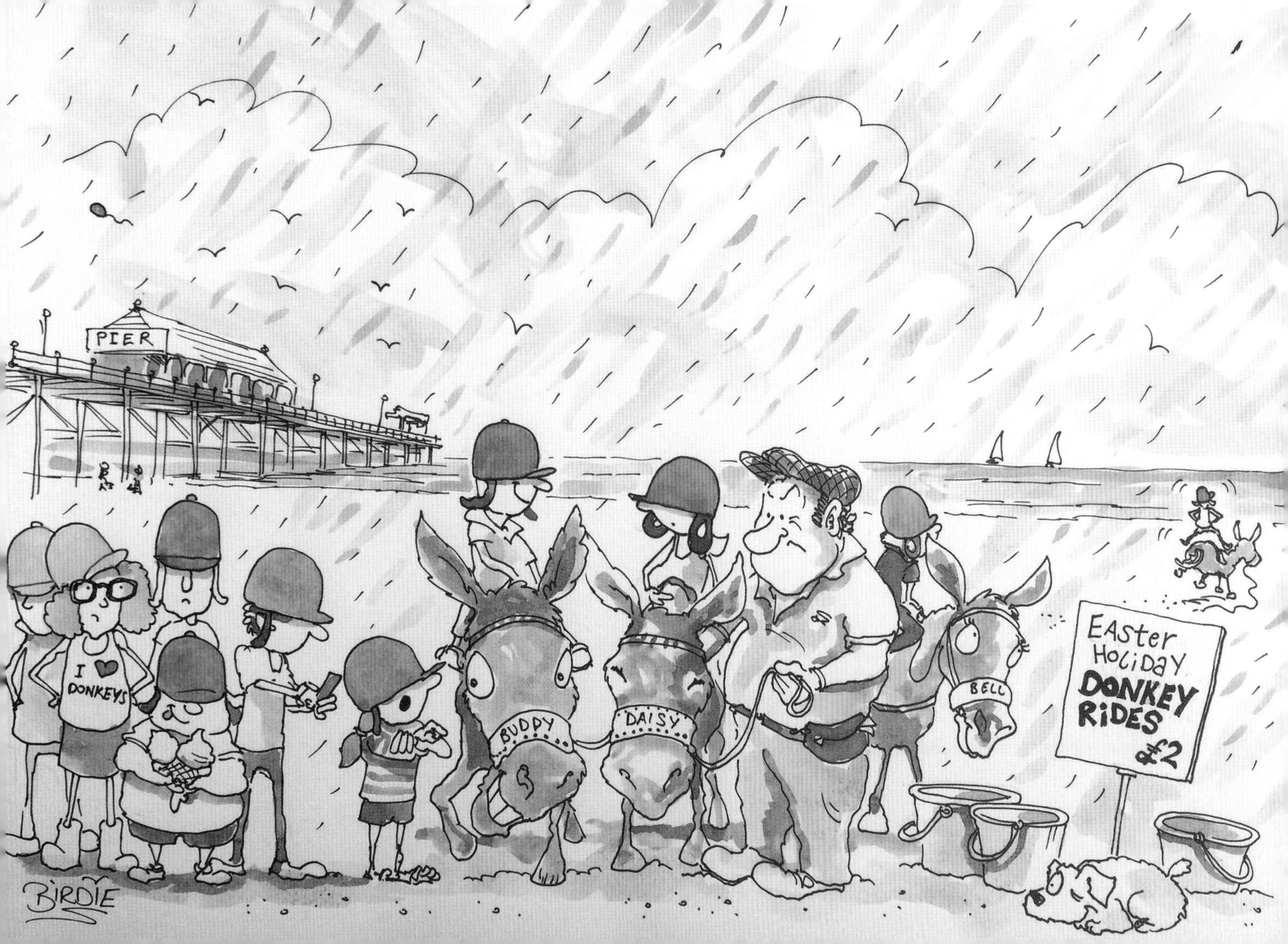
PIER
I ♥ DONKEYS
BUDDY
DAISY
BELL
EASTER HOLIDAY DONKEY RIDES £2
BIRDIE

Prince Charles' Irish visit to Sligo

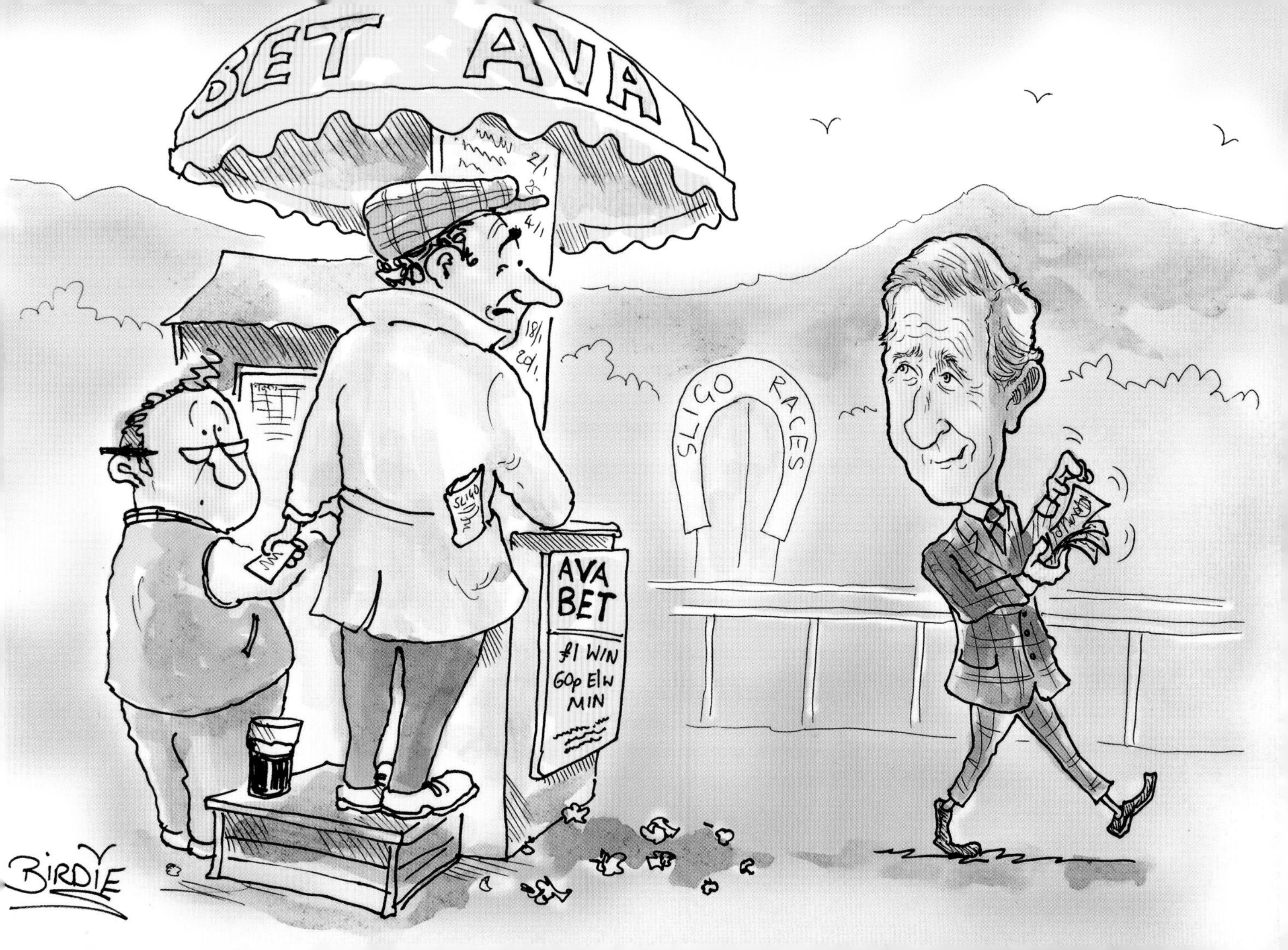
BET AVA
2/1
4/1
18/1
20/1
SLIGO
SLIGO RACES
AVA BET
£1 WIN
60p E/W
MIN
BIRDIE

D. Biro 2013

Seagull weather

Opposite: It was freezing
at Southwell

Racing on the frozen lake at St Moritz

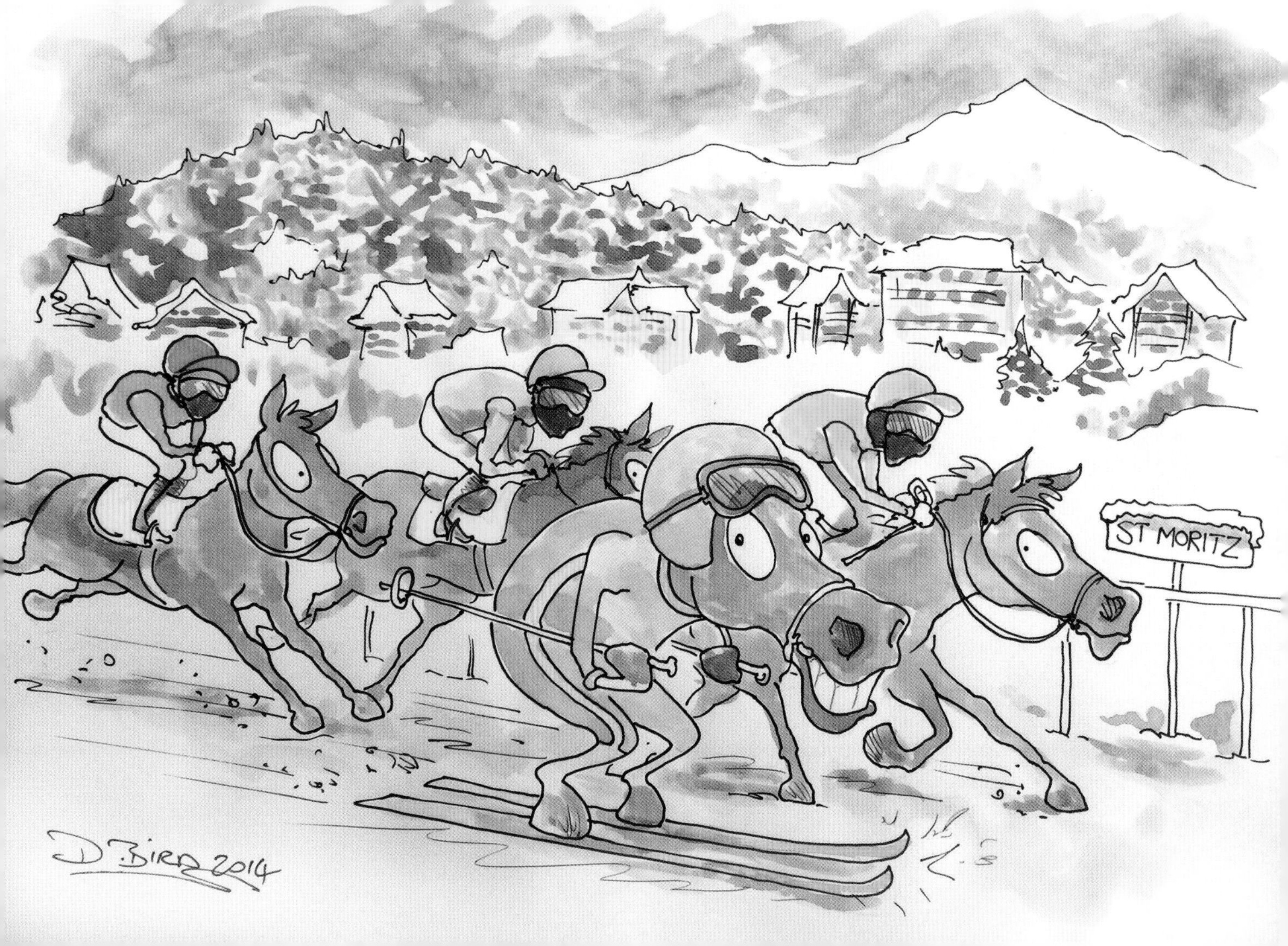
ST MORITZ
D. BIRD 2014

Balthazar King recovers from his fall in the 2015 Grand National

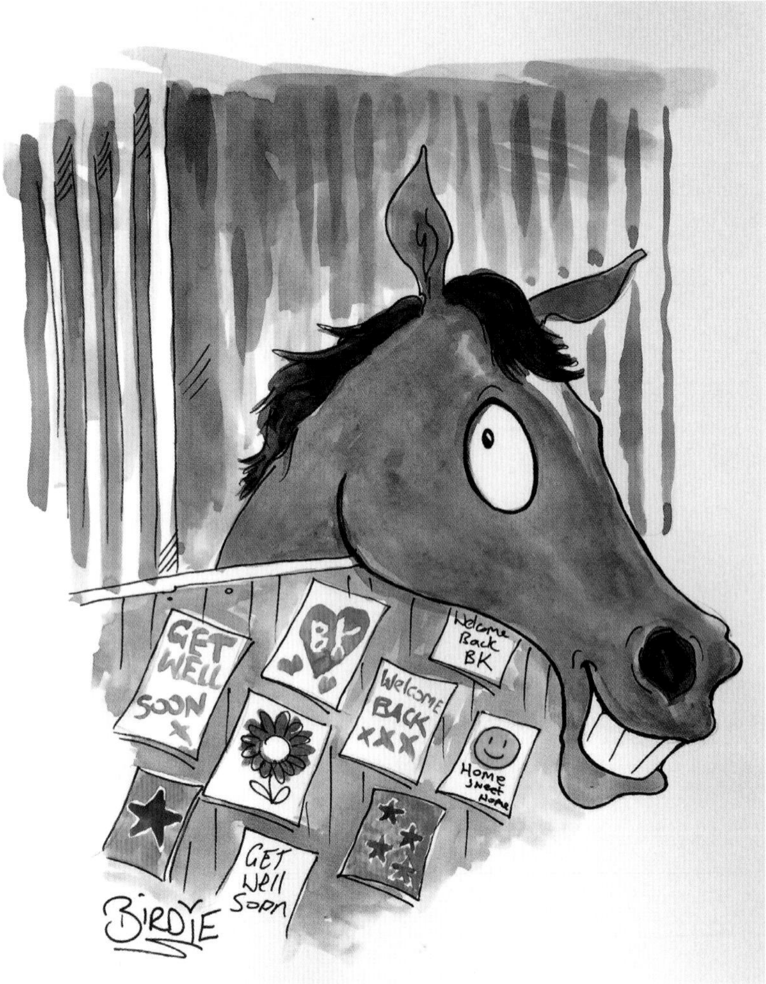
GET WELL SOON x
BK
Welcome Back BK
Welcome BACK xxx
Home Sweet Home
GET Well Soon
BIRDIE

MOONEE VALLEY
THE CLEANER
D BIRD 2014

The Cleaner mops up another race Down Under

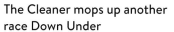

Trainer Roger Varian ensures Kingston Hill
has ideal ground for the St Leger

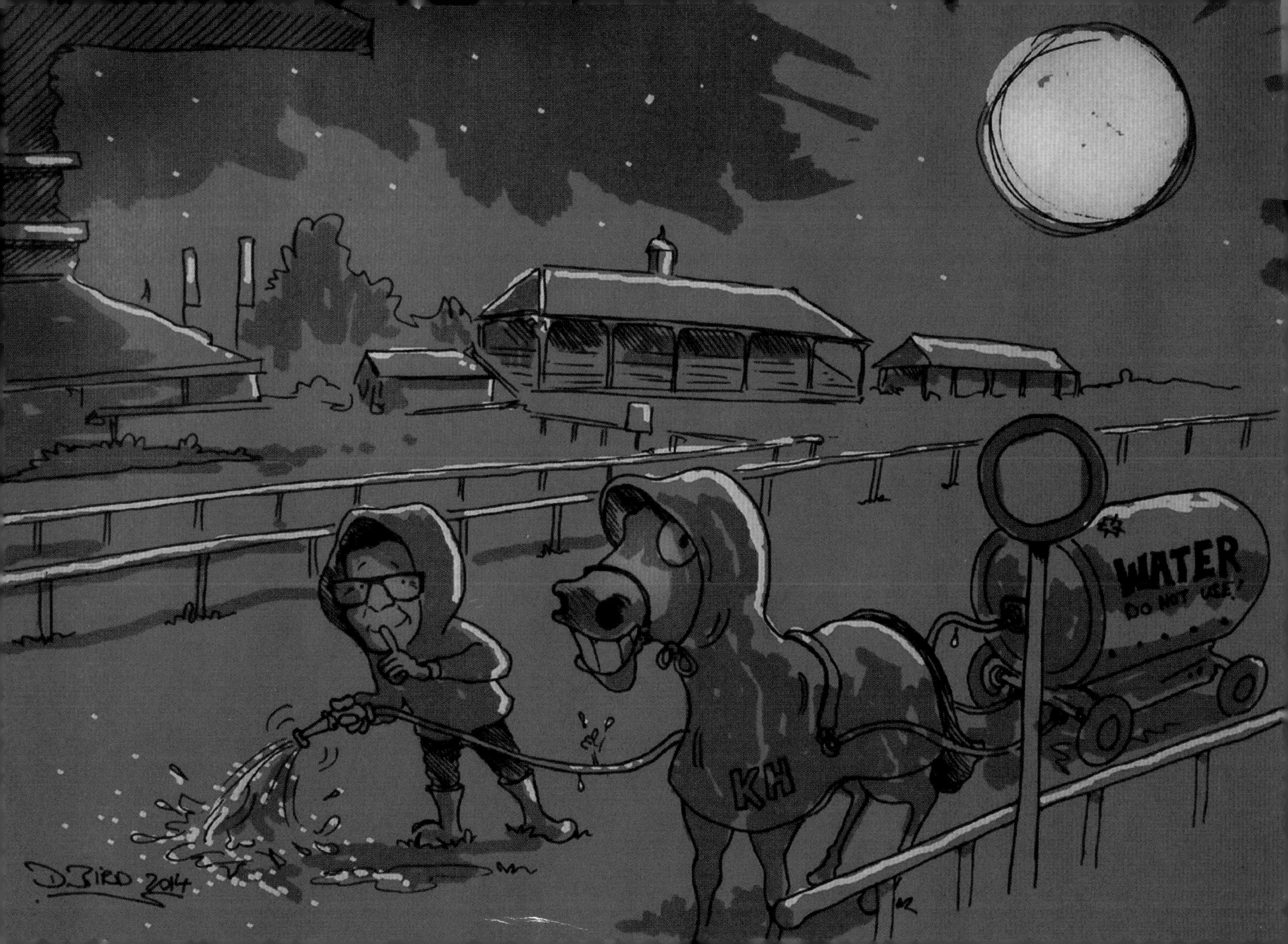
WATER
DO NOT USE!
KH
D.BIRD 2014

Happy Halloween
from Birdie

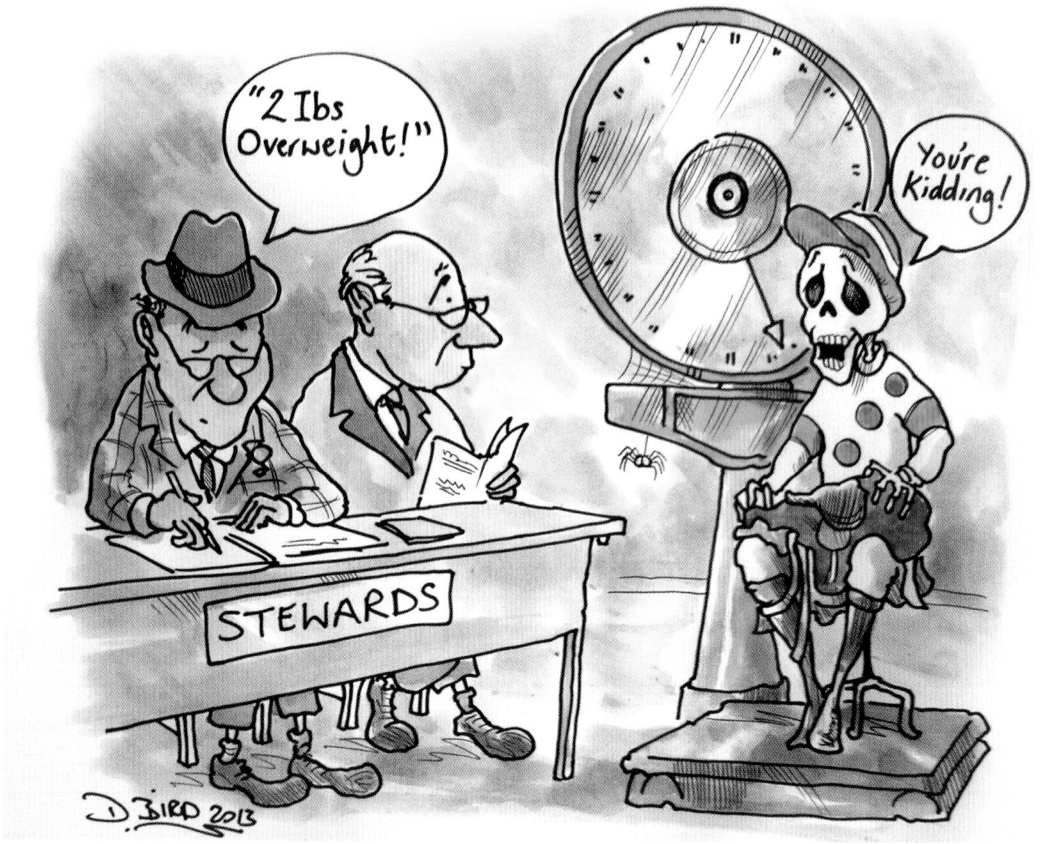
"2 lbs Overweight!"
You're Kidding!
STEWARDS
D. BIRD 2013

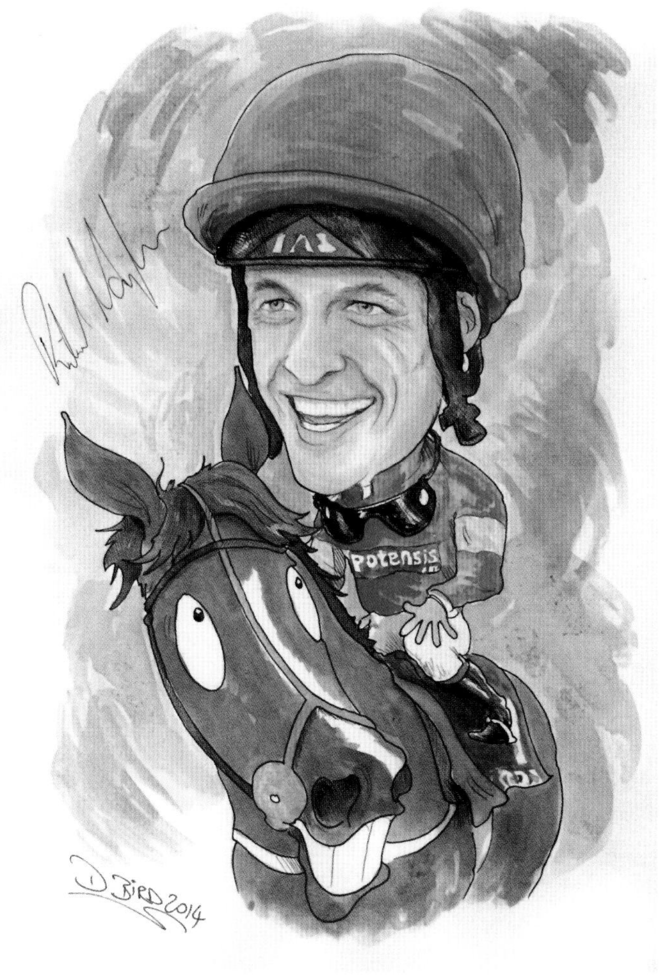
Potensis
D BIRD 2014

Richard Hughes and Tiggy Wiggy make Lowther Stakes smiles at York

American Pharoah wins the Triple Crown
for Victor Espinoza and Bob Baffert

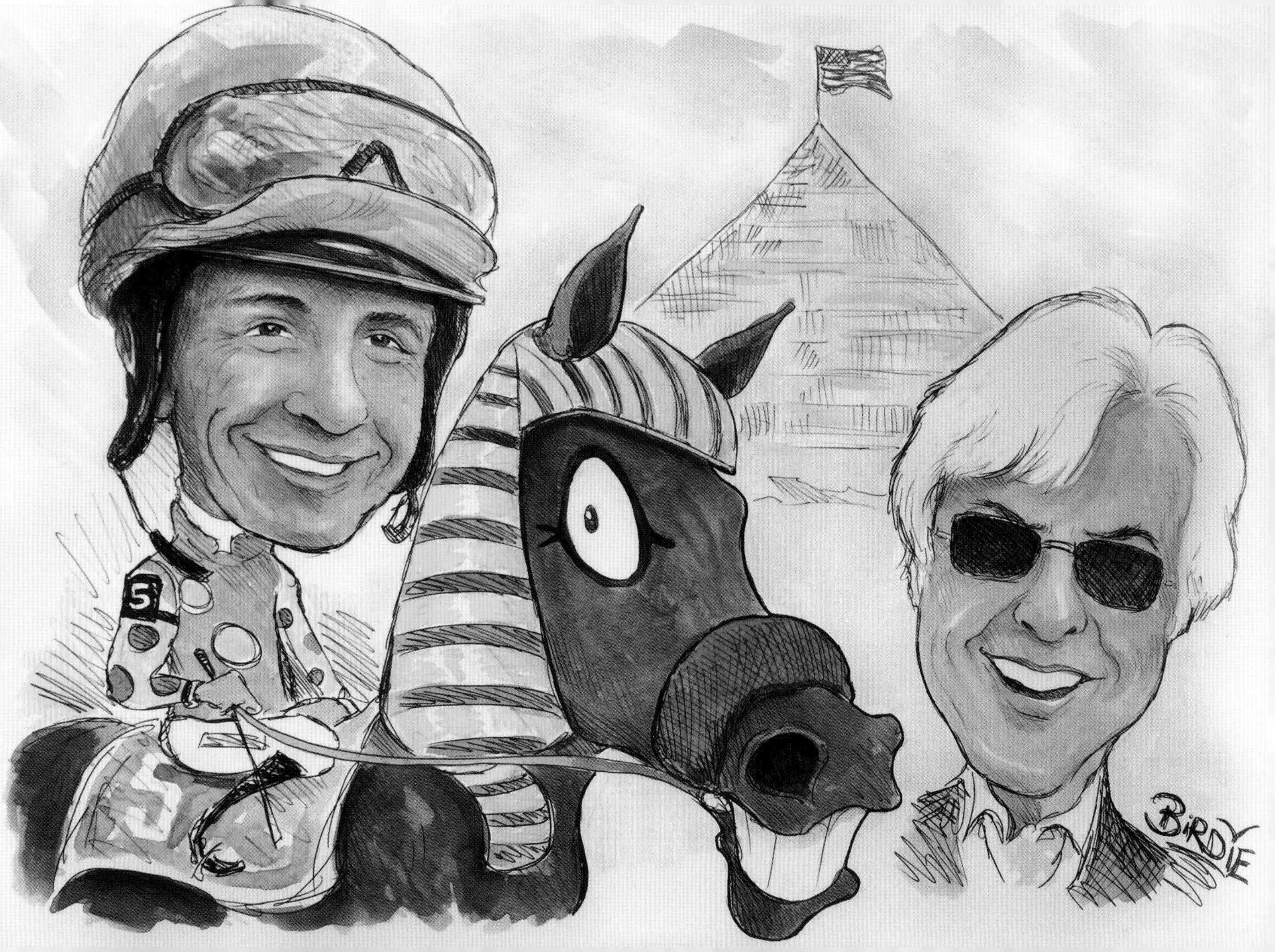
5
BiRDIE

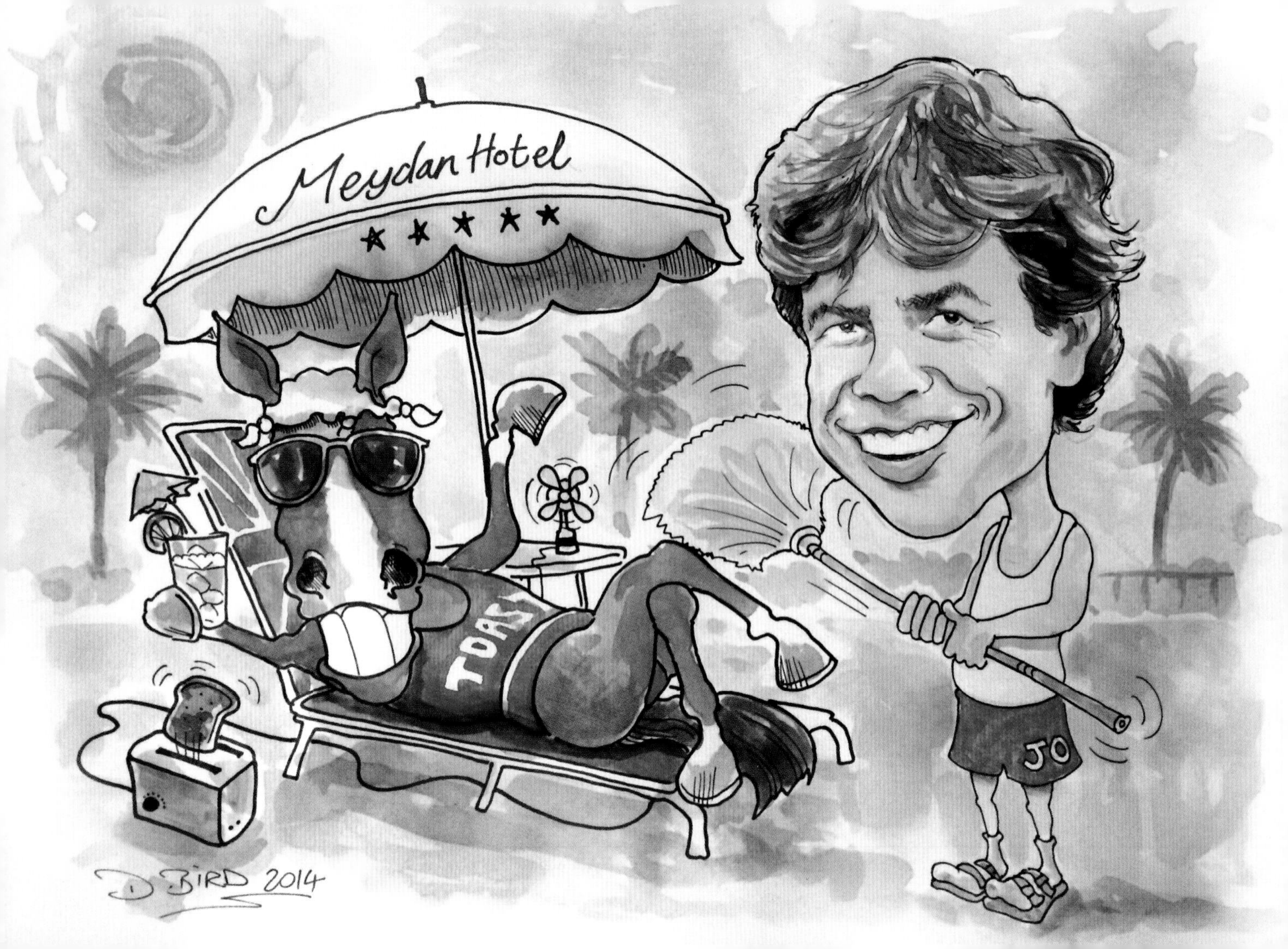

Meydan Hotel
TOAST
JO
D BIRD 2014

Jamie Osborne is Toast Of New York's biggest fan after the UAE Derby at Meydan

Ascot winner Dartmouth sails away
in the royal colours

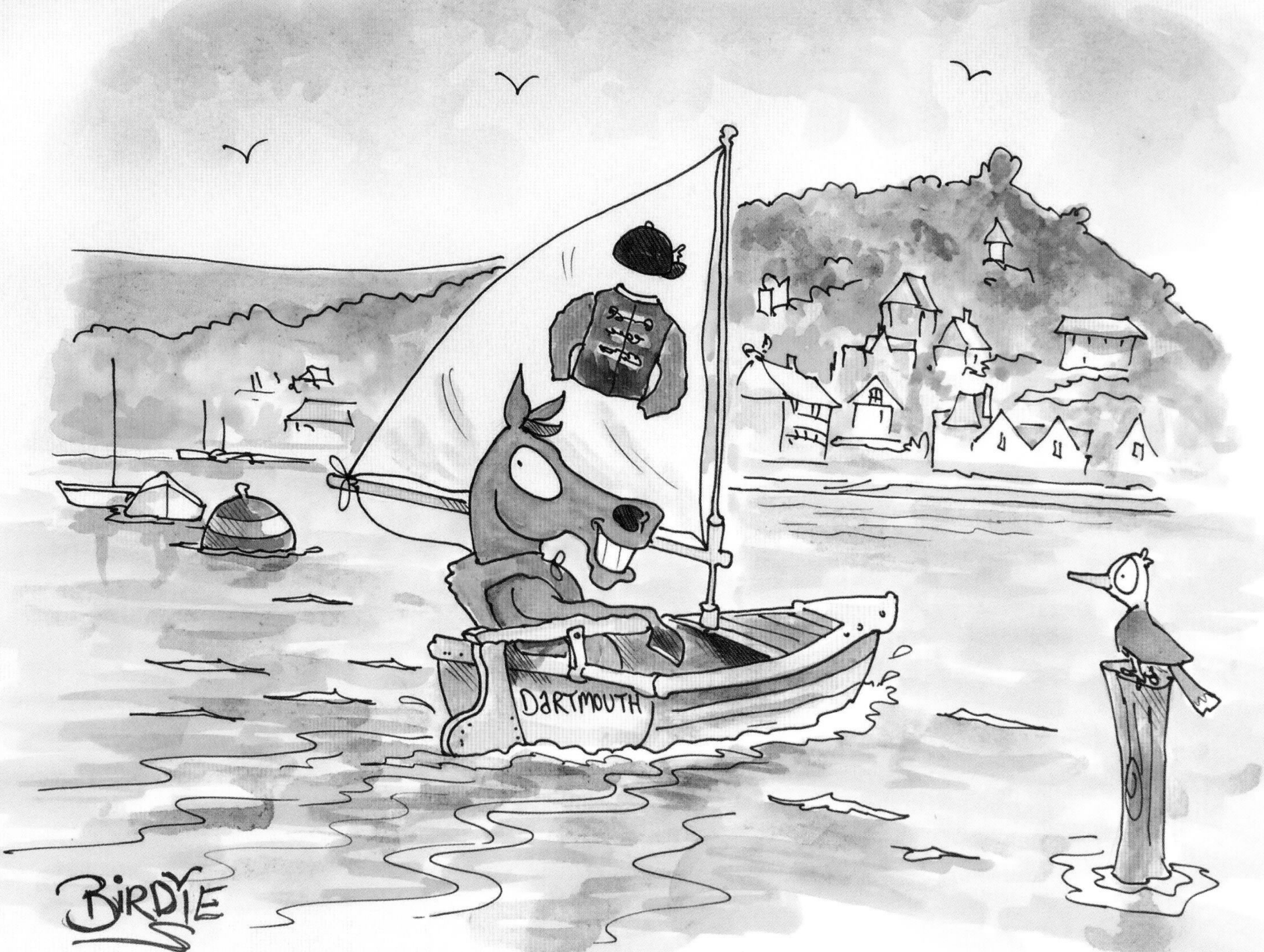
DARTMOUTH
BIRDIE

Volume arrives at the start of the Irish Oaks in the wrong shoes

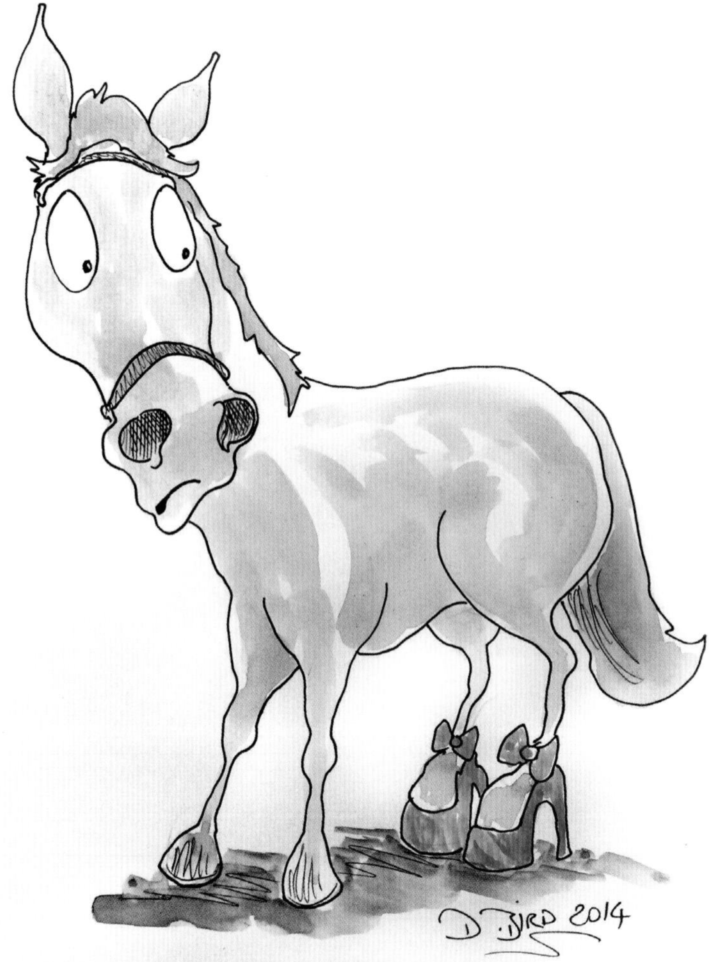
D. BIRD 2014

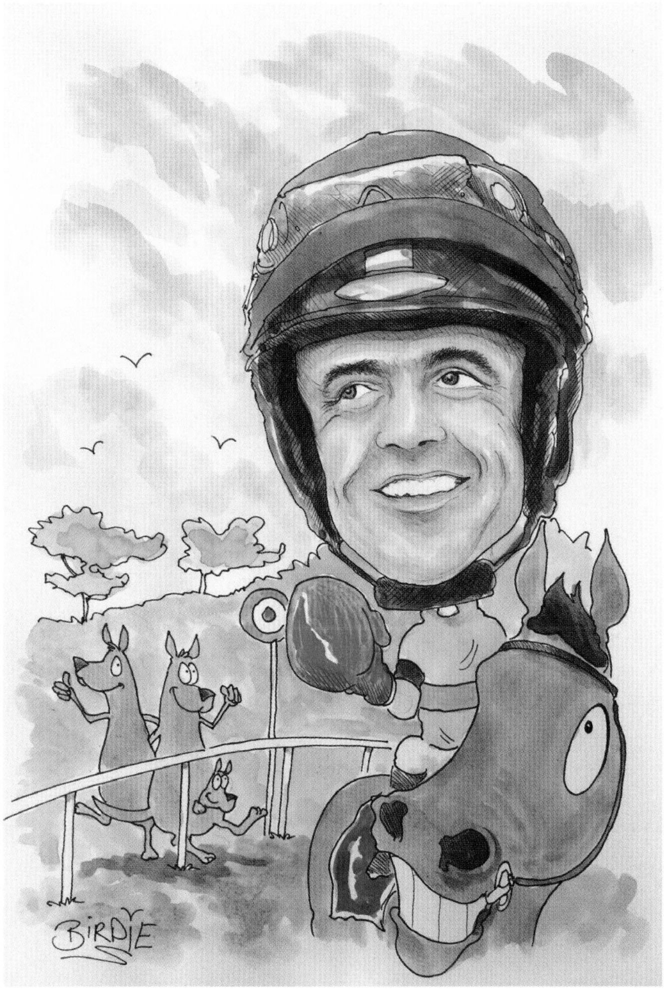
BIRDIE

Ruby Walsh goes Down Under to win the Australian Grand National on Bashboy

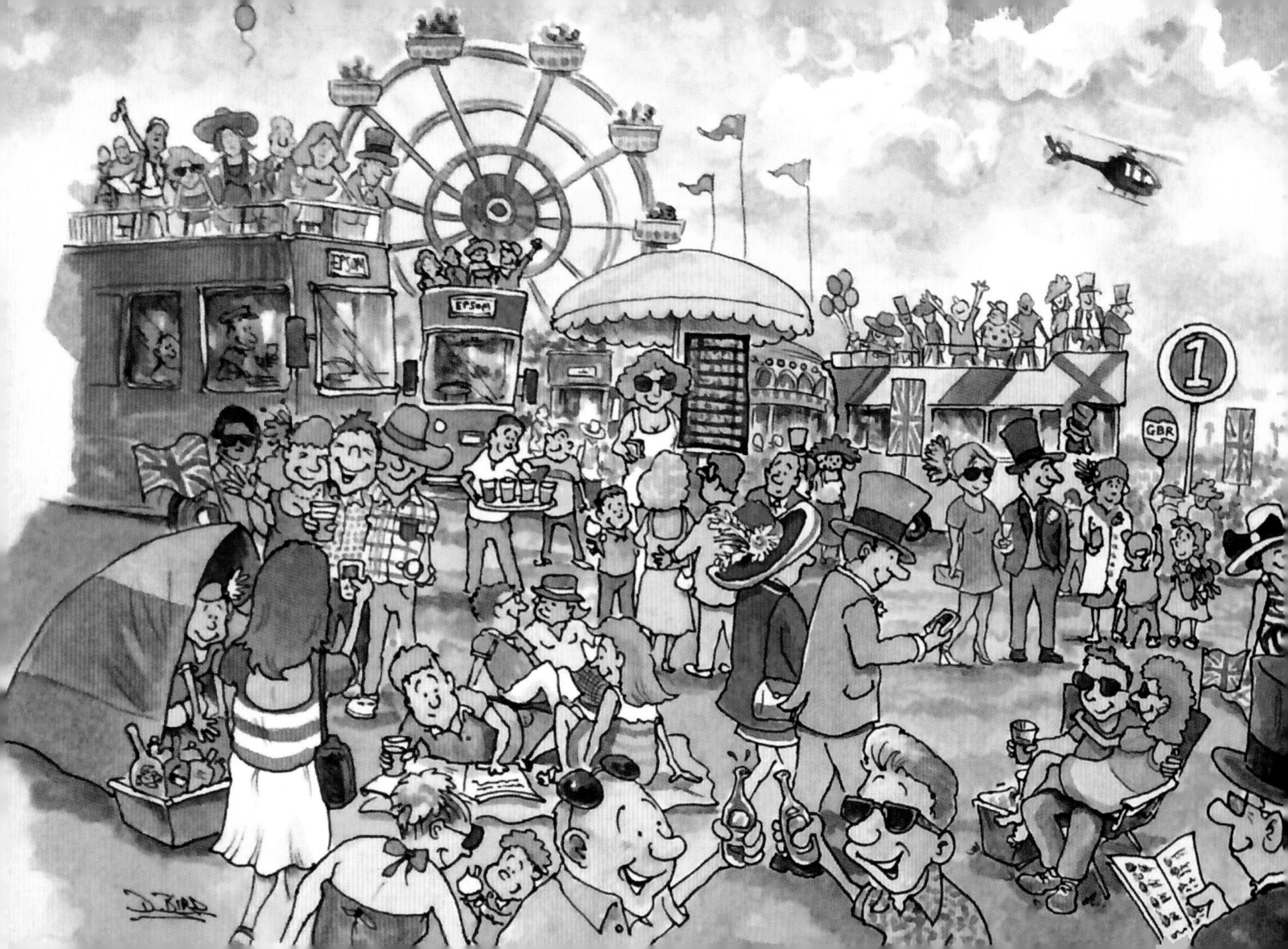
EPSOM
EPSOM
1
GBR

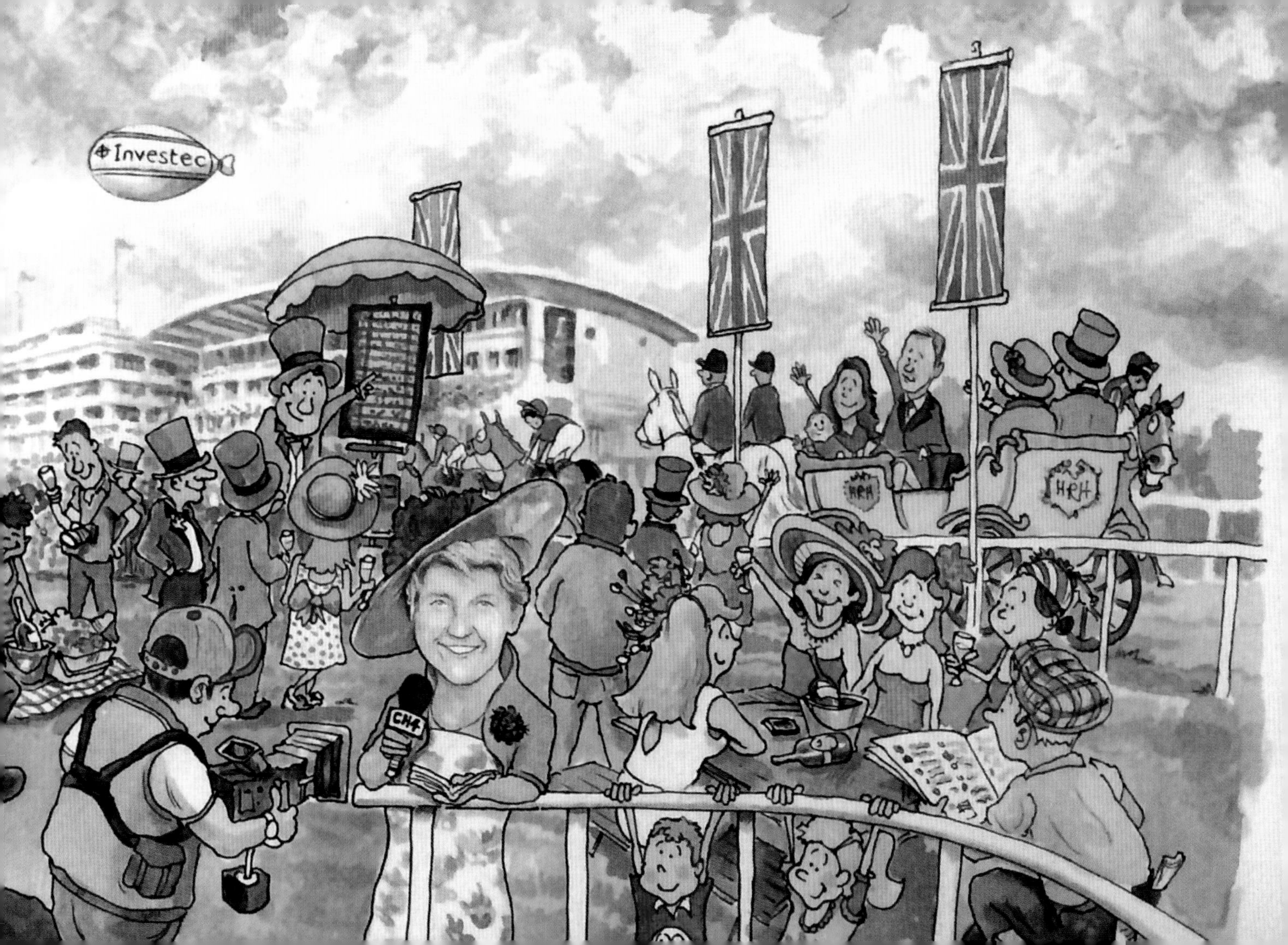
Investec
CH4
HRH
HRH

Previous: Birdie's modern version of Frith's
classic painting, The Derby Day

Opposite: 'Neigh-bours' – Kylie at the races

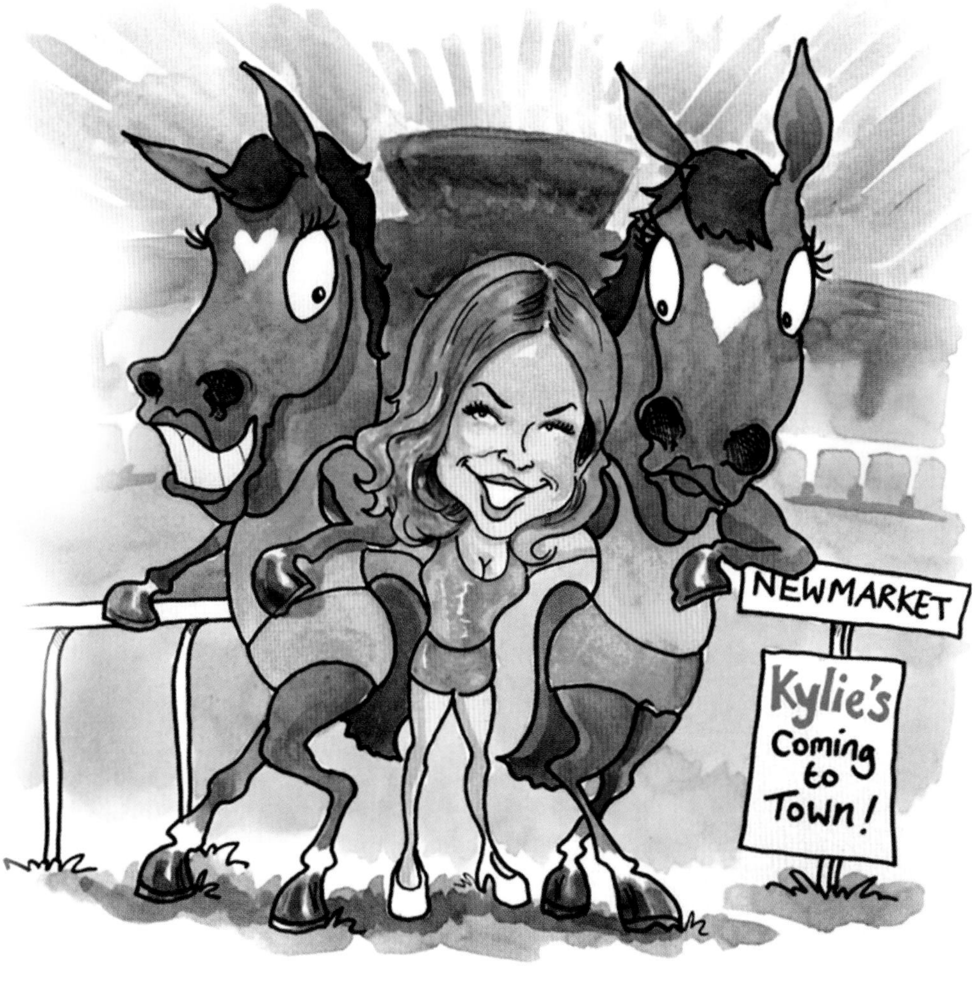
NEWMARKET
Kylie's Coming to Town!

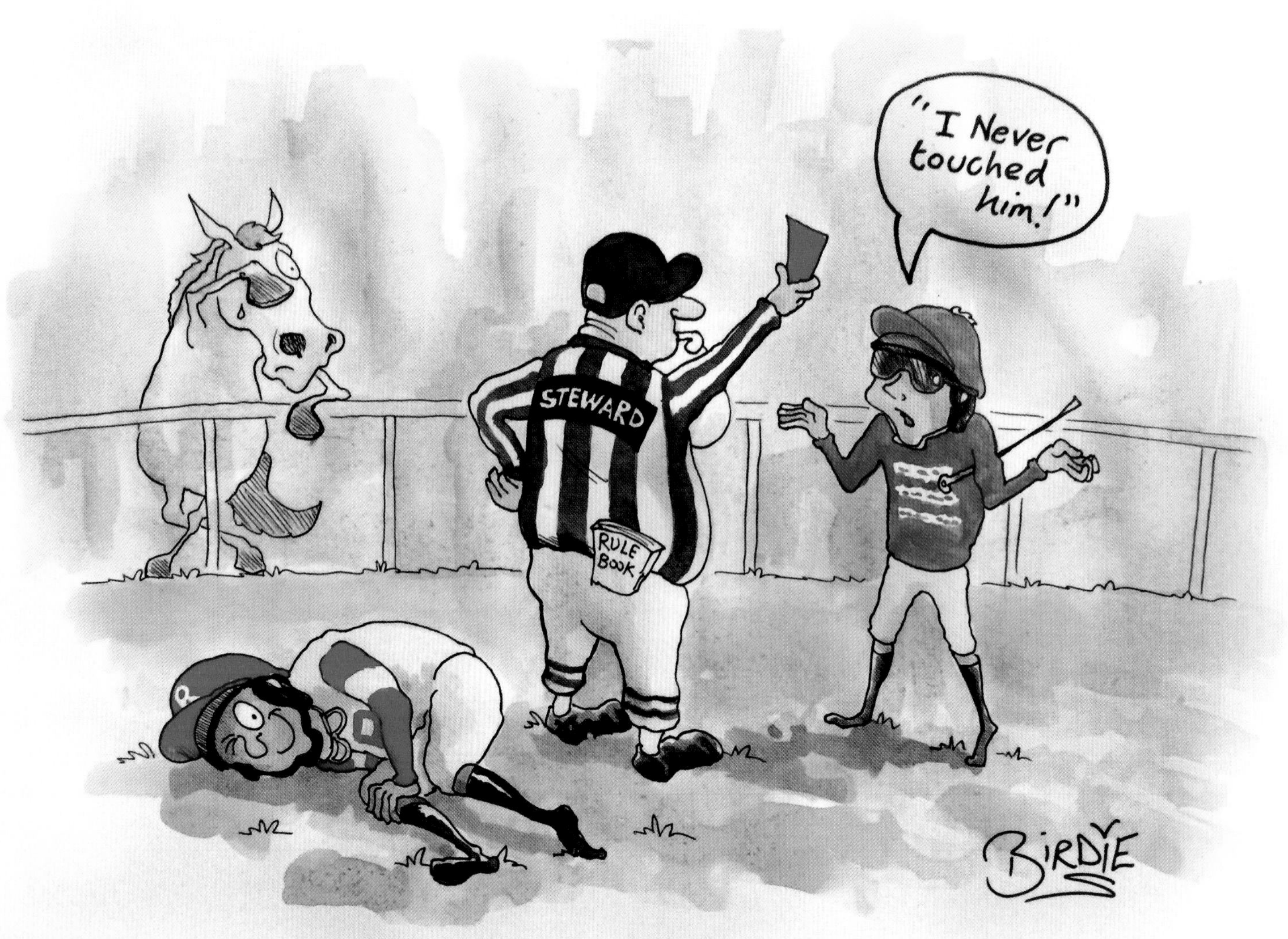
"I Never touched him!"
STEWARD
RULE BOOK
BIRDIE

Chicago stewards disqualify British raiders Secret Gesture and Jamie Spencer after local rider does a 'dying swan'

Festival dreams

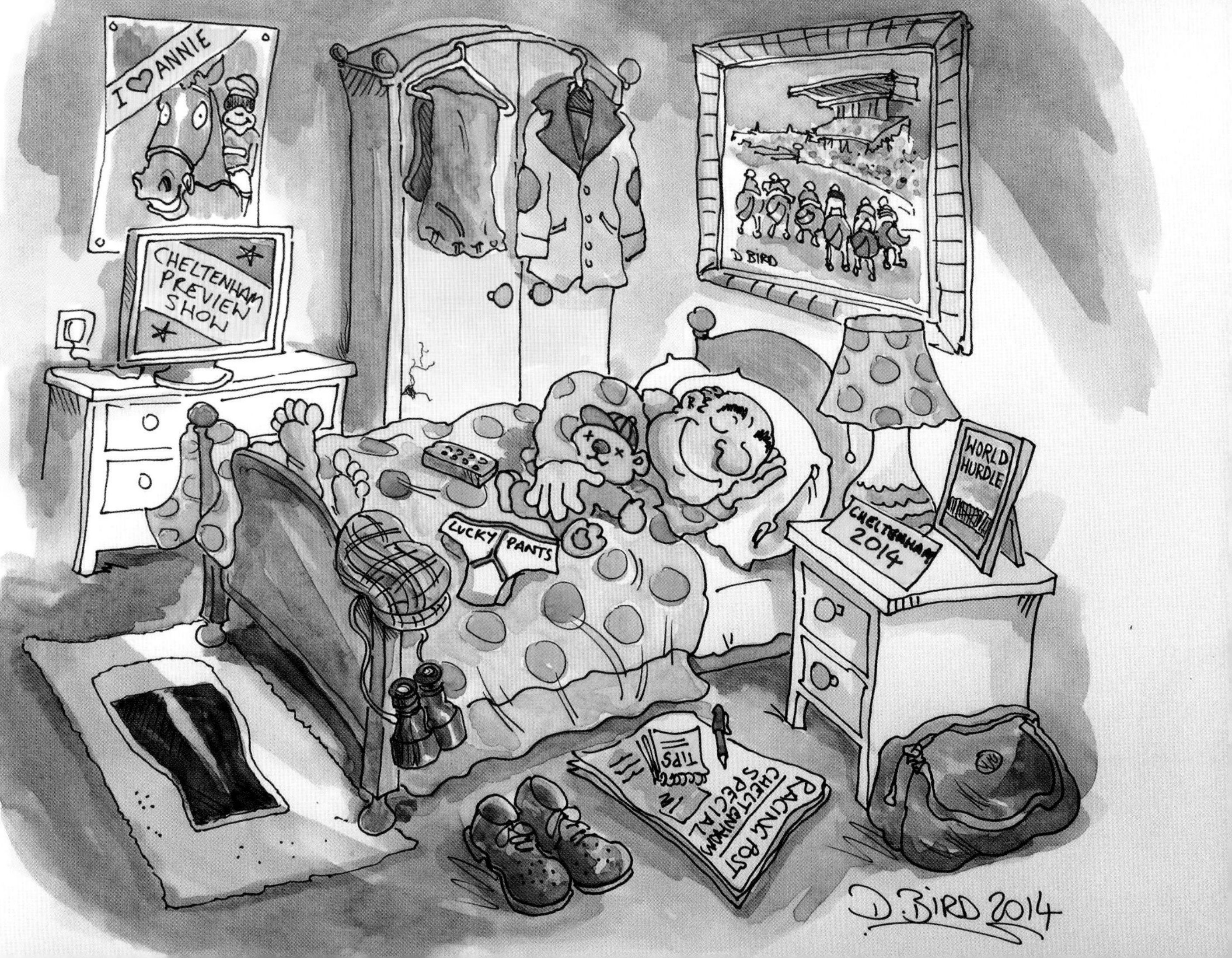
I ♥ ANNIE
CHELTENHAM PREVIEW SHOW
D BIRD
WORLD HURDLE
CHELTENHAM 2014
LUCKY PANTS
RACING POST
CHELTENHAM SPECIAL
TIPS
D.BIRD 2014

A horse called Father Christmas
runs at Royal Ascot

Guinness cheekpieces –
a must-have for St Patrick's Day

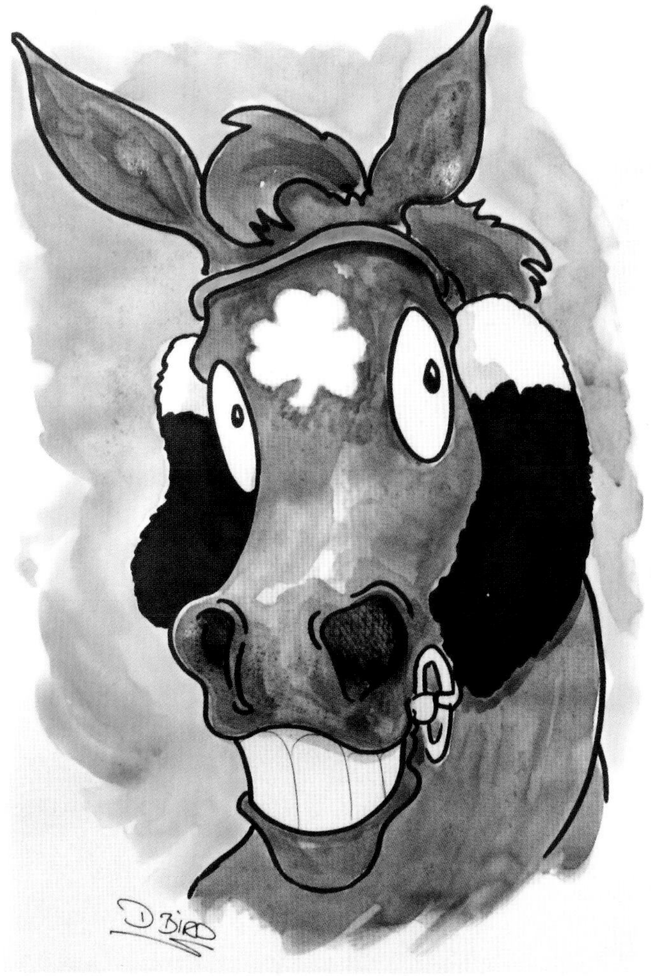
D BIRD

Oliver Sherwood on cloud nine after Many
Clouds wins the Hennessy Gold Cup

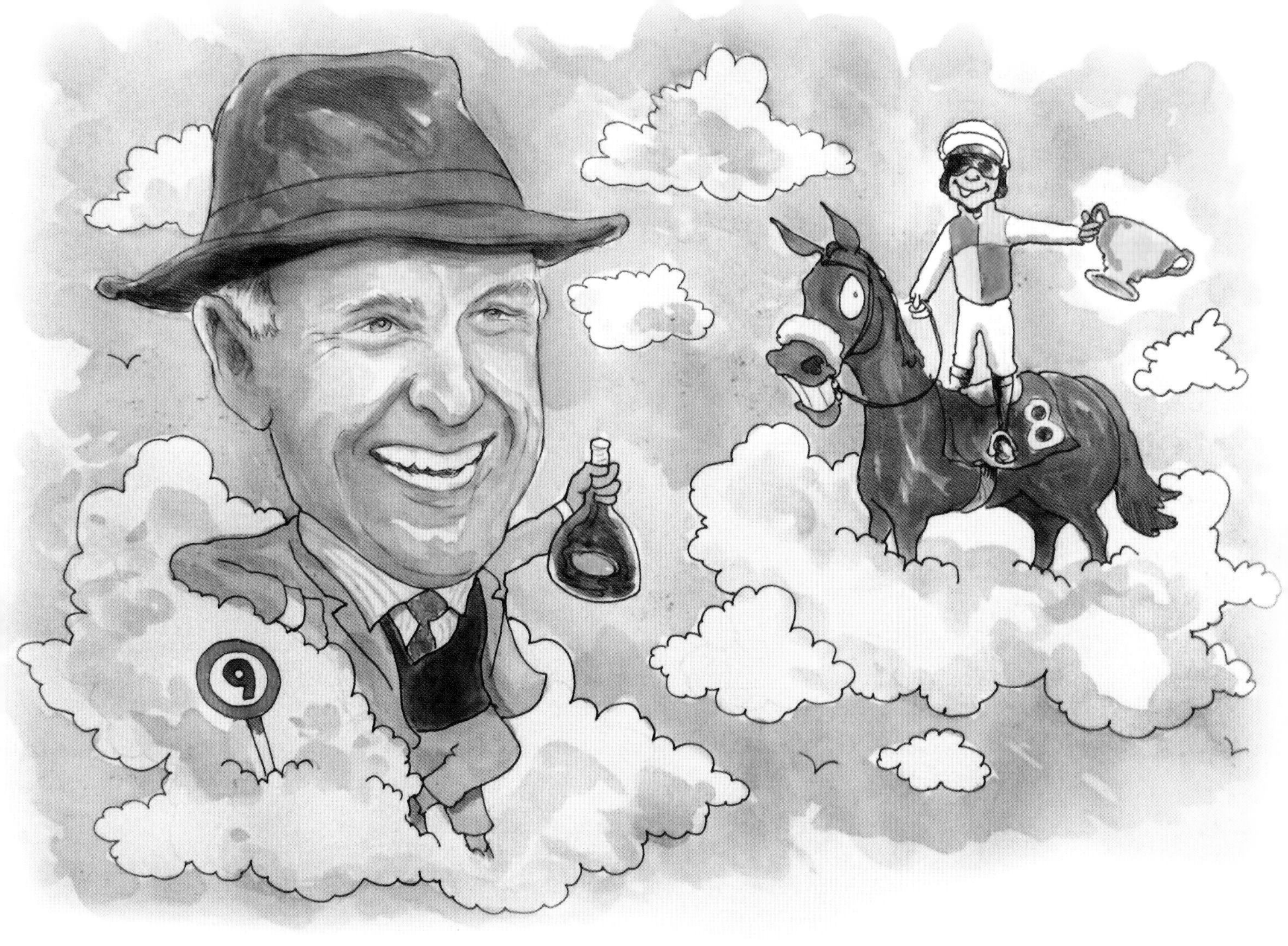
9
8

Easter Bunnies

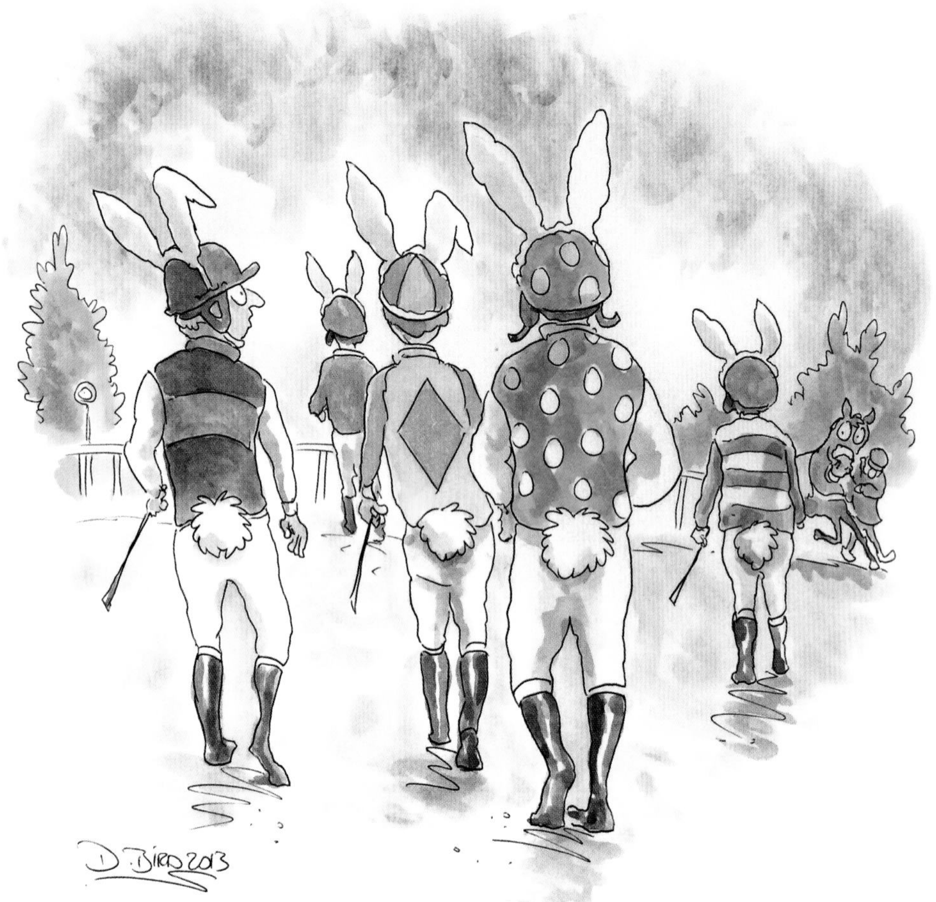
D. BIRD 2013

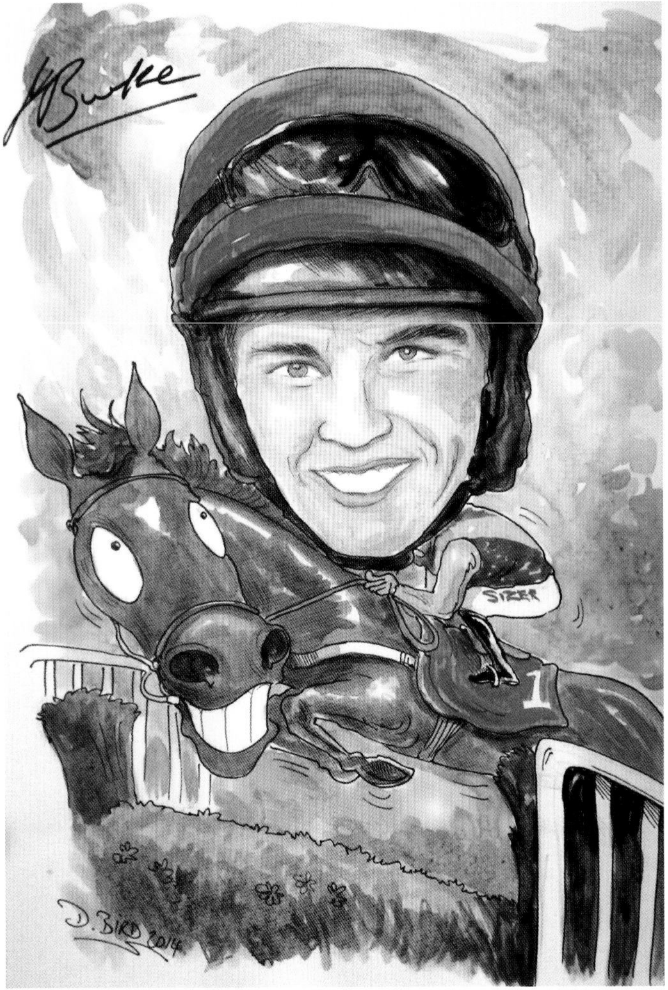
SIZER
D. BIRD 2014

Young Jonathan Burke wins the Midlands Grand National on Goonyella

Three Kings at Kempton – King George VI Chase winners
Long Run, Silviniaco Conti and Kauto Star

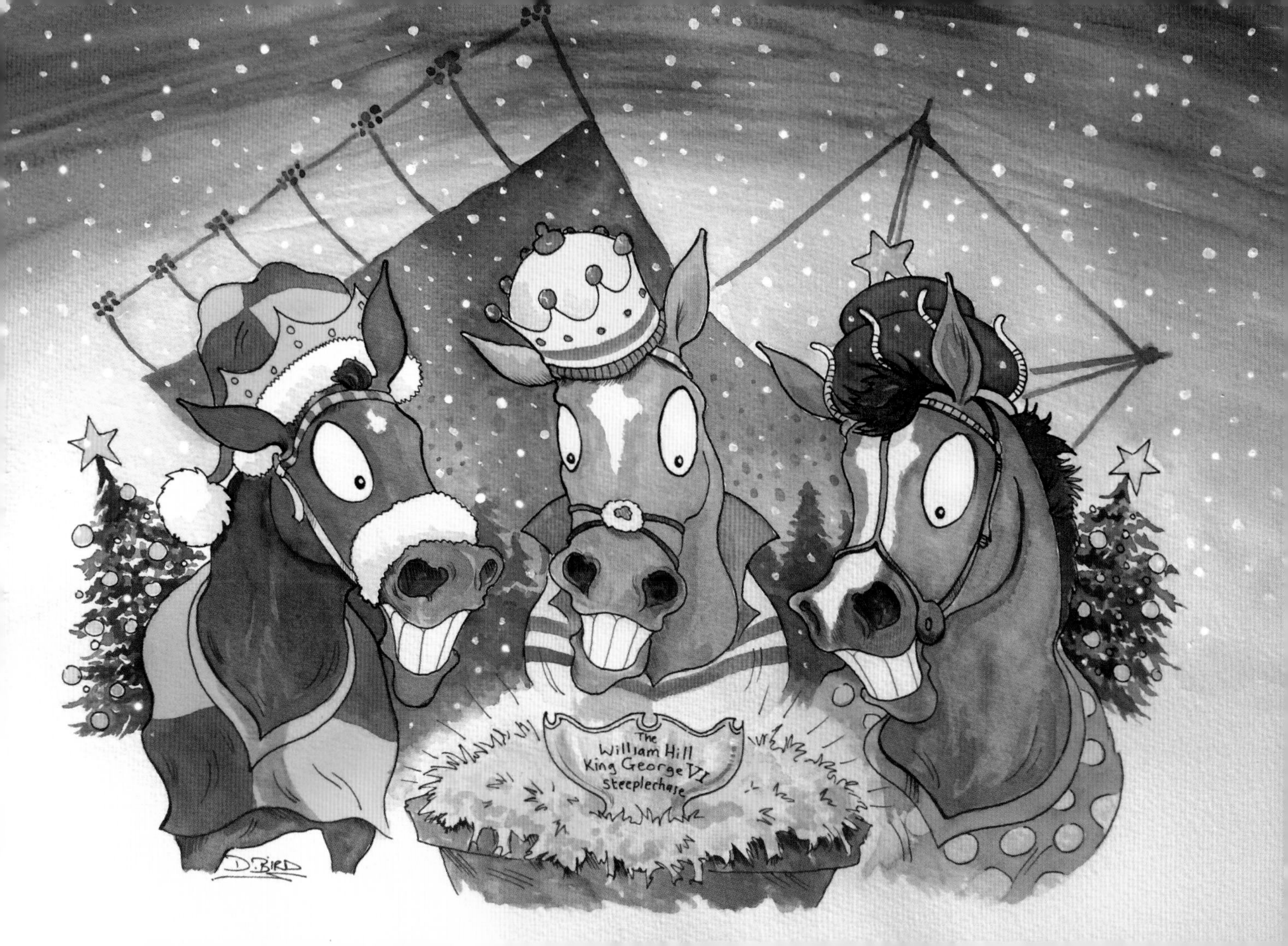
The William Hill King George VI steeplechase
D. BIRD

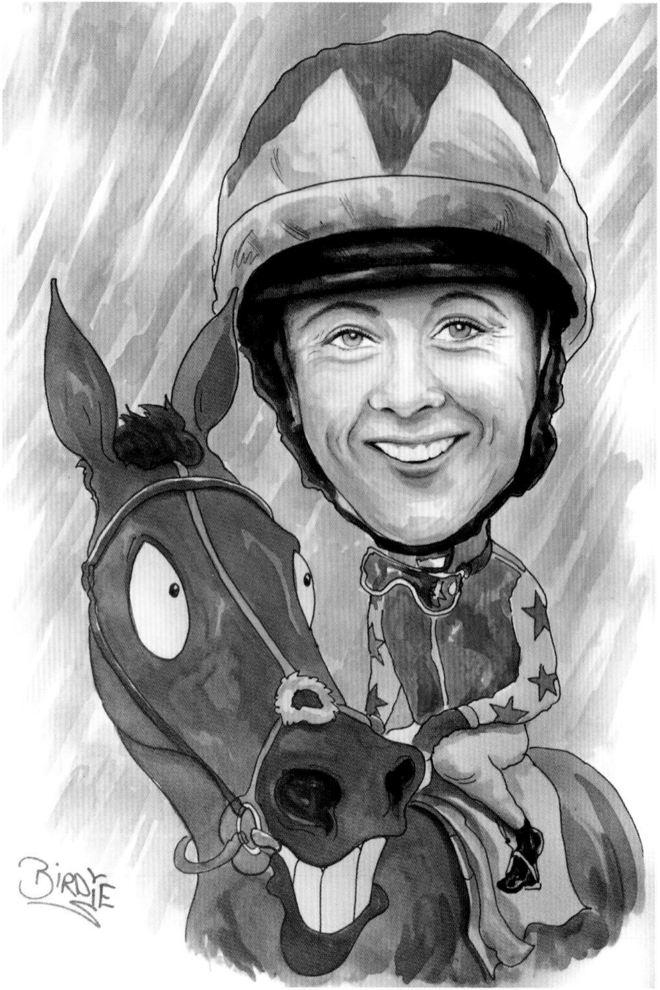
BIRDIE

Hayley Turner wins on Roudee at the Roodee, Chester

Barry Geraghty on his 2013
Gold Cup winner Bobs Worth

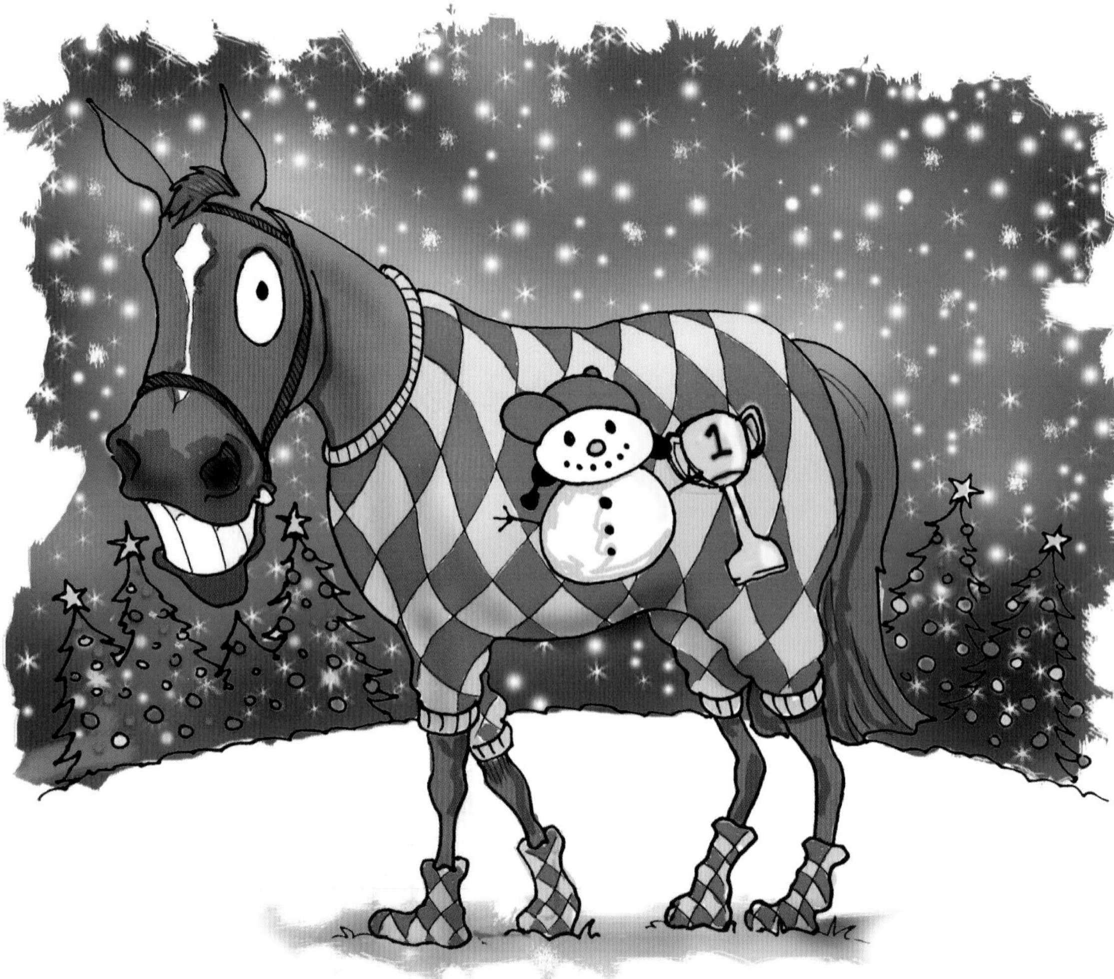
1

Red Cadeaux sends 'Seasonal Greetings' – Ed Dunlop commissioned Birdie for his Christmas card

Frankie blows the horn at Epsom

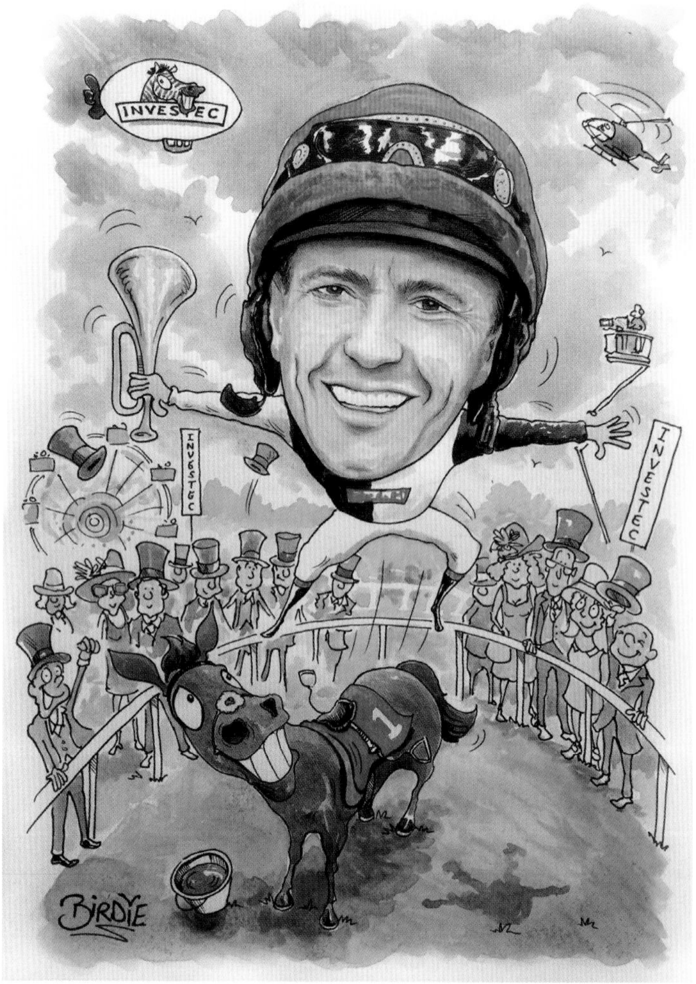
INVESTEC
INVESTEC
INVESTEC
1
BIRDIE

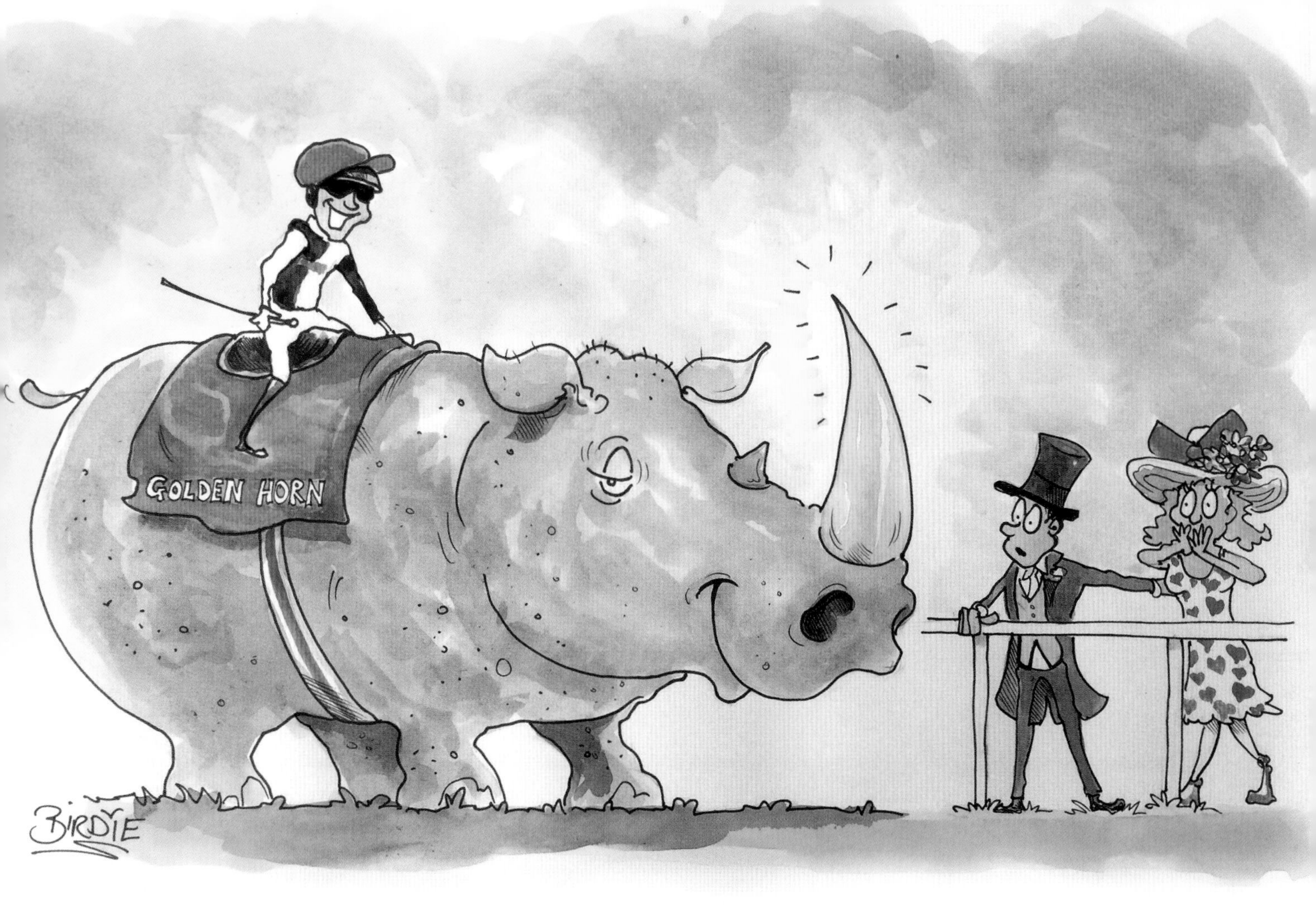
GOLDEN HORN
BIRDIE

Perfect Gentleman shows his manners at Cheltenham

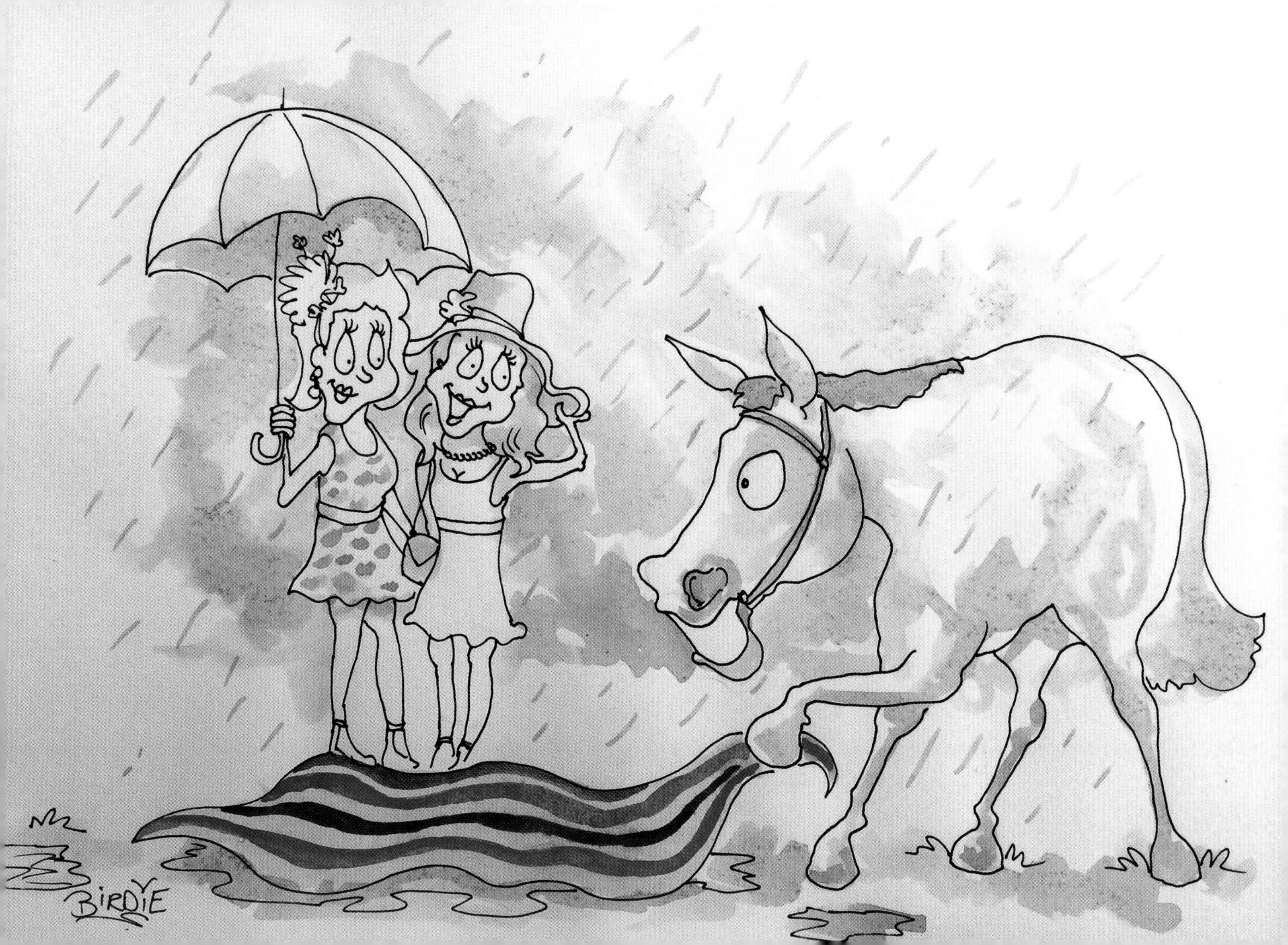
BIRDIE

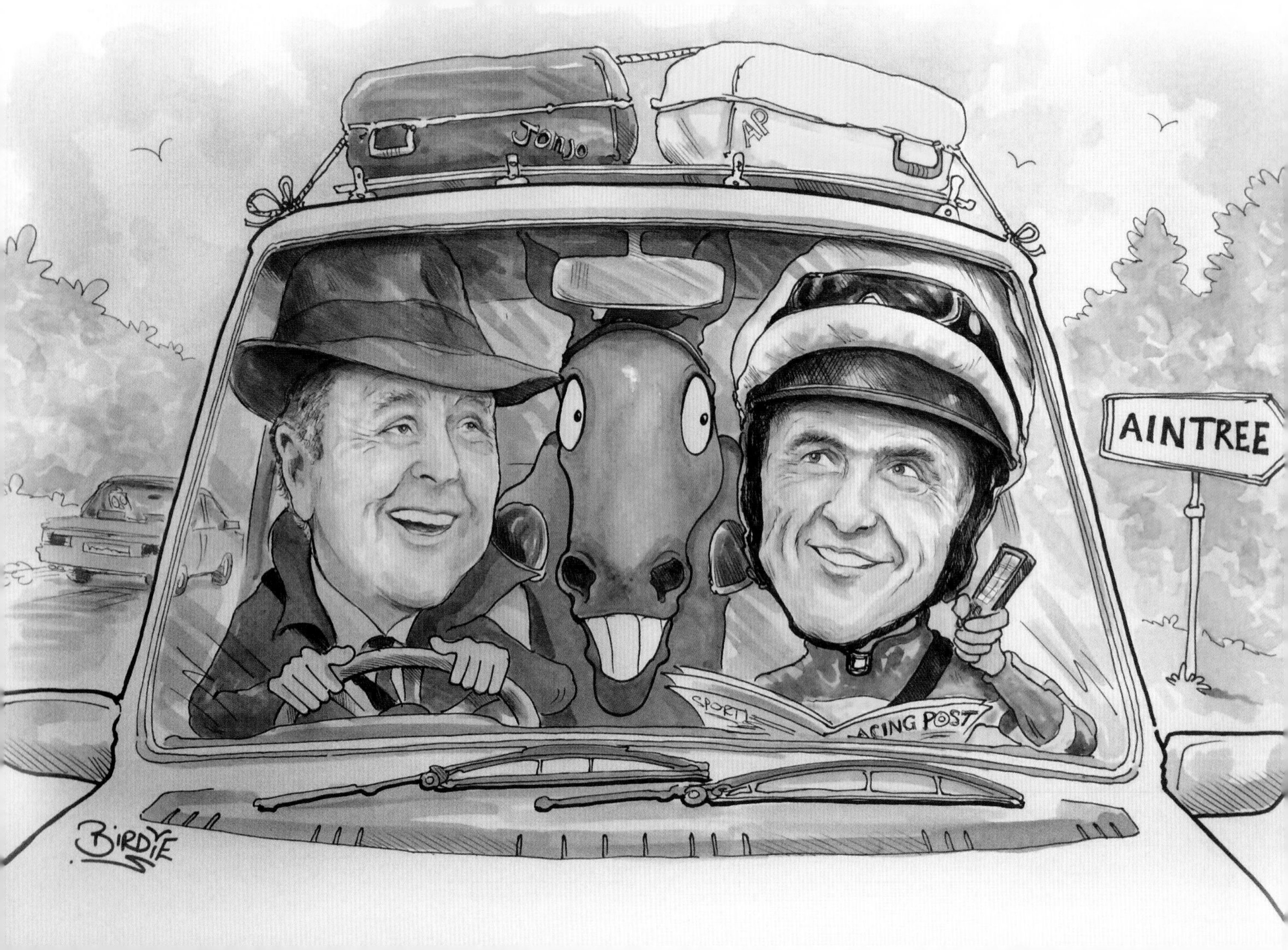
JONJO
AP
AINTREE
SPORT
ACING POST
BIRDIE

'Who forgot to Shutthefrontdoor?' – AP McCoy's last ride in the Grand National and Birdie's first cartoon in the *Racing Post*

Farewell AP McCoy – Sandown Park, 25 April 2015

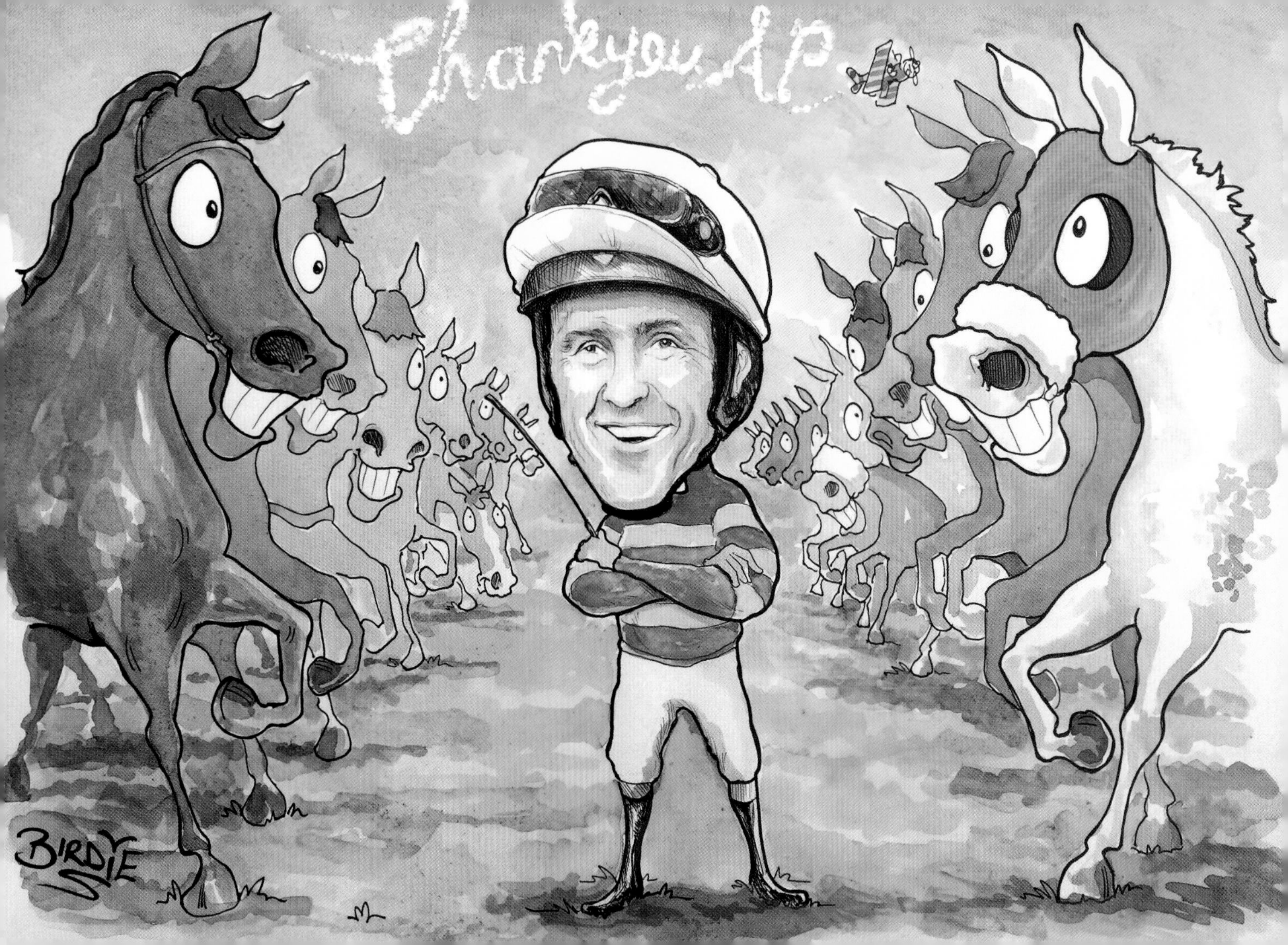
Thankyou AP
BIRDIE

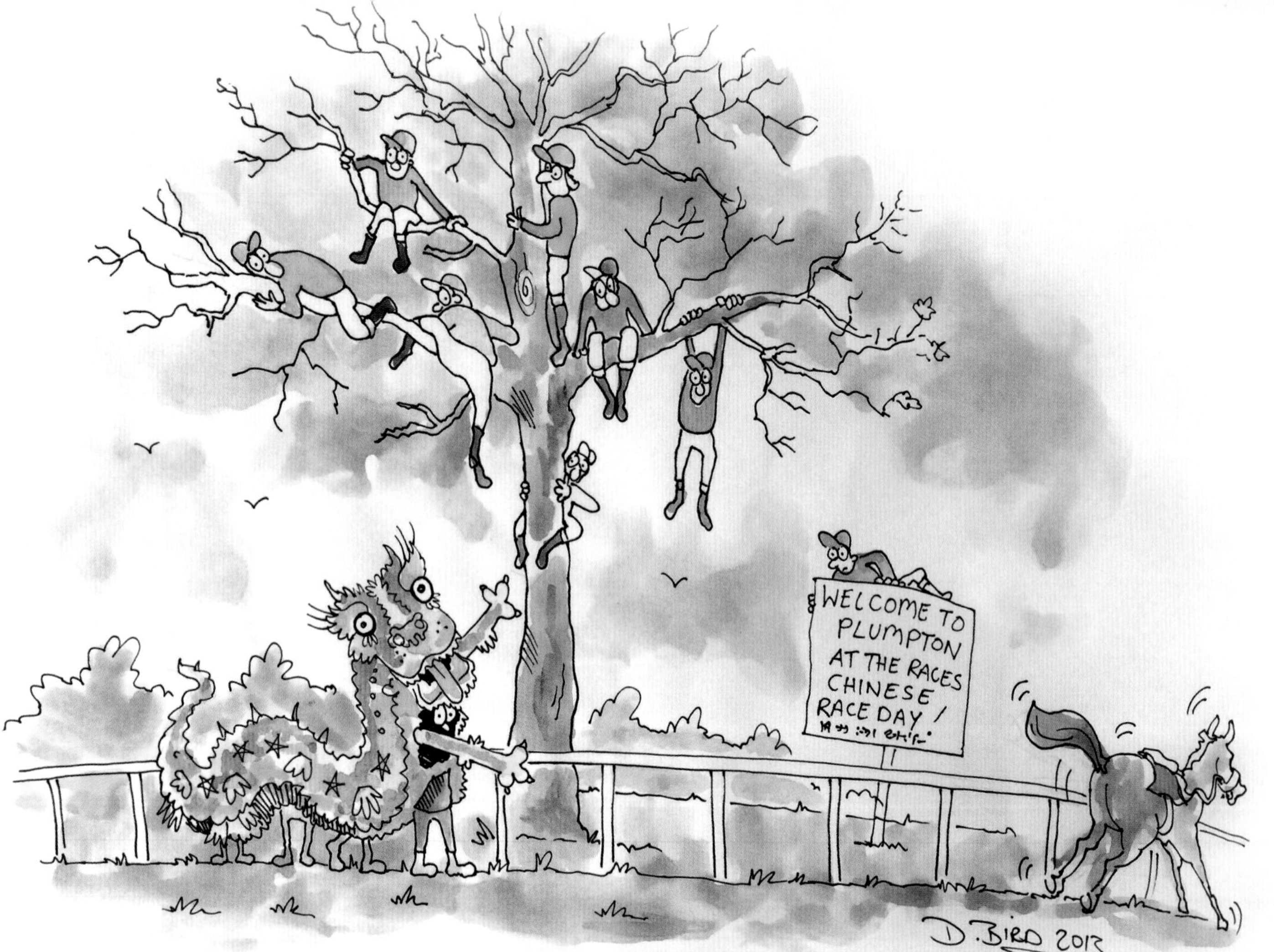
WELCOME TO
PLUMPTON
AT THE RACES
CHINESE
RACE DAY!
D. BIRD 2013

Treble up. Aidan Coleman and Venetia Williams celebrate three winners at Sandown

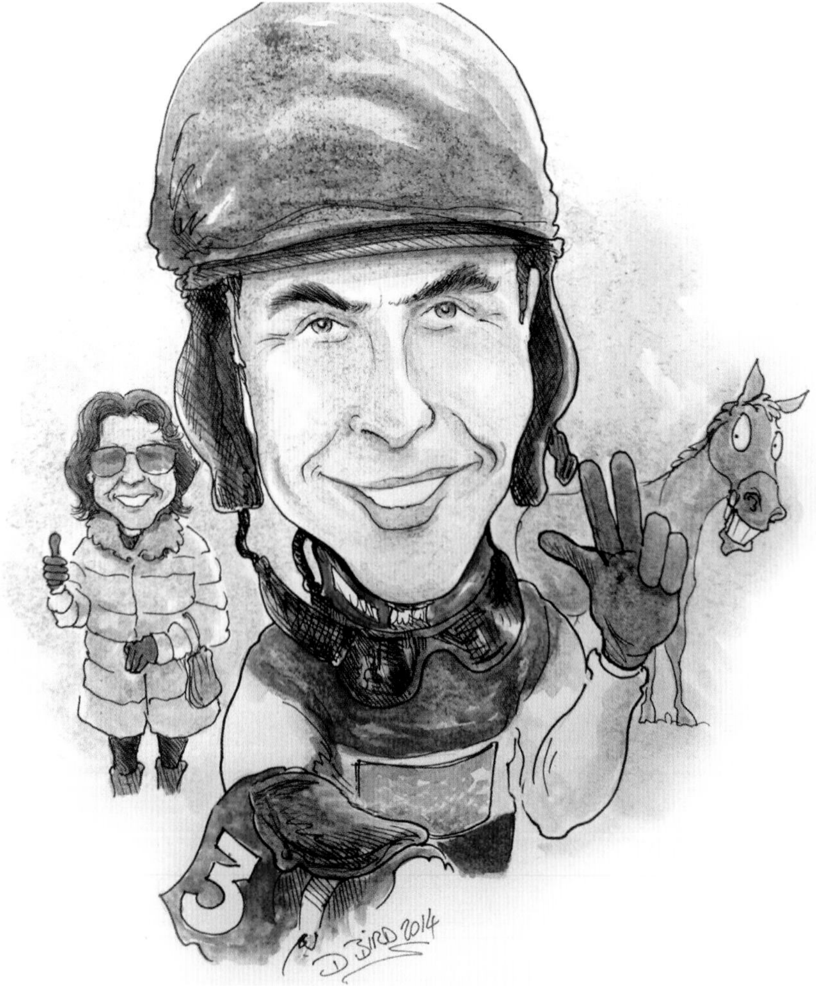
3
D BIRD 2014

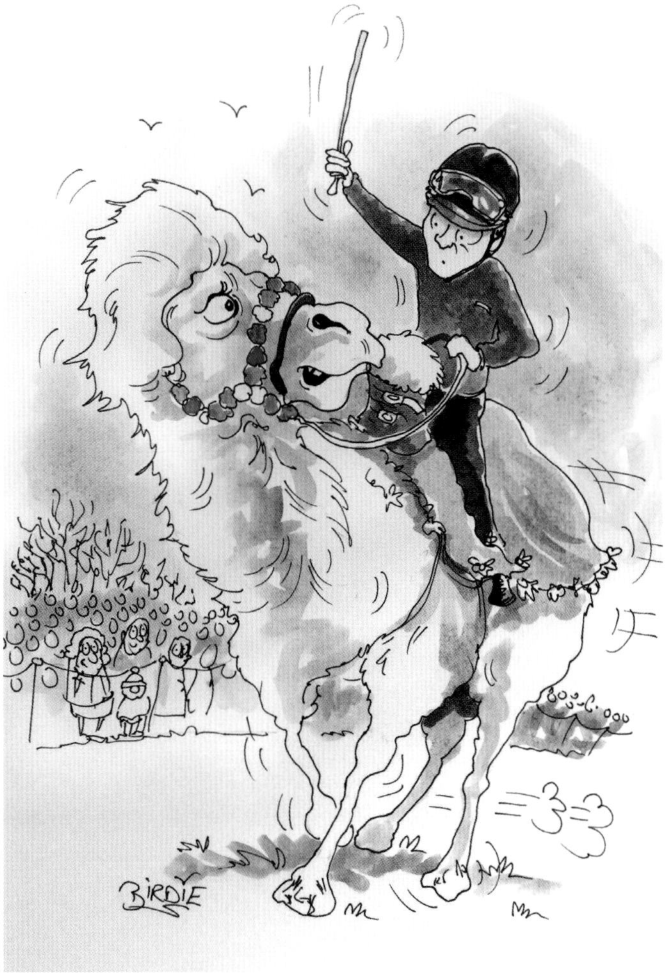
BIRDIE

'Don't get the hump with me!' – Camels come to Lambourn Open Day

King Of Rooks flies high at Sandown

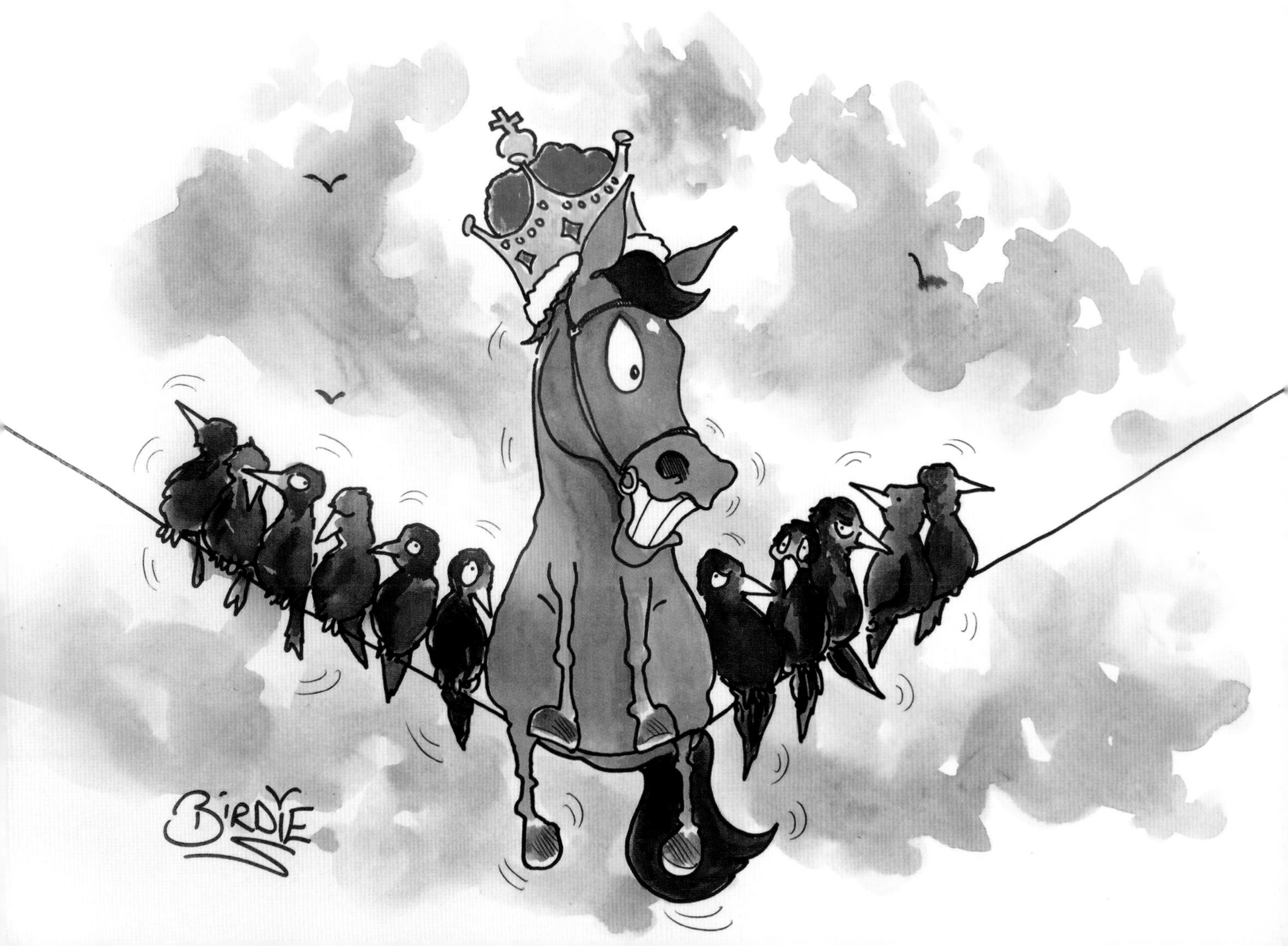
BIRDIE

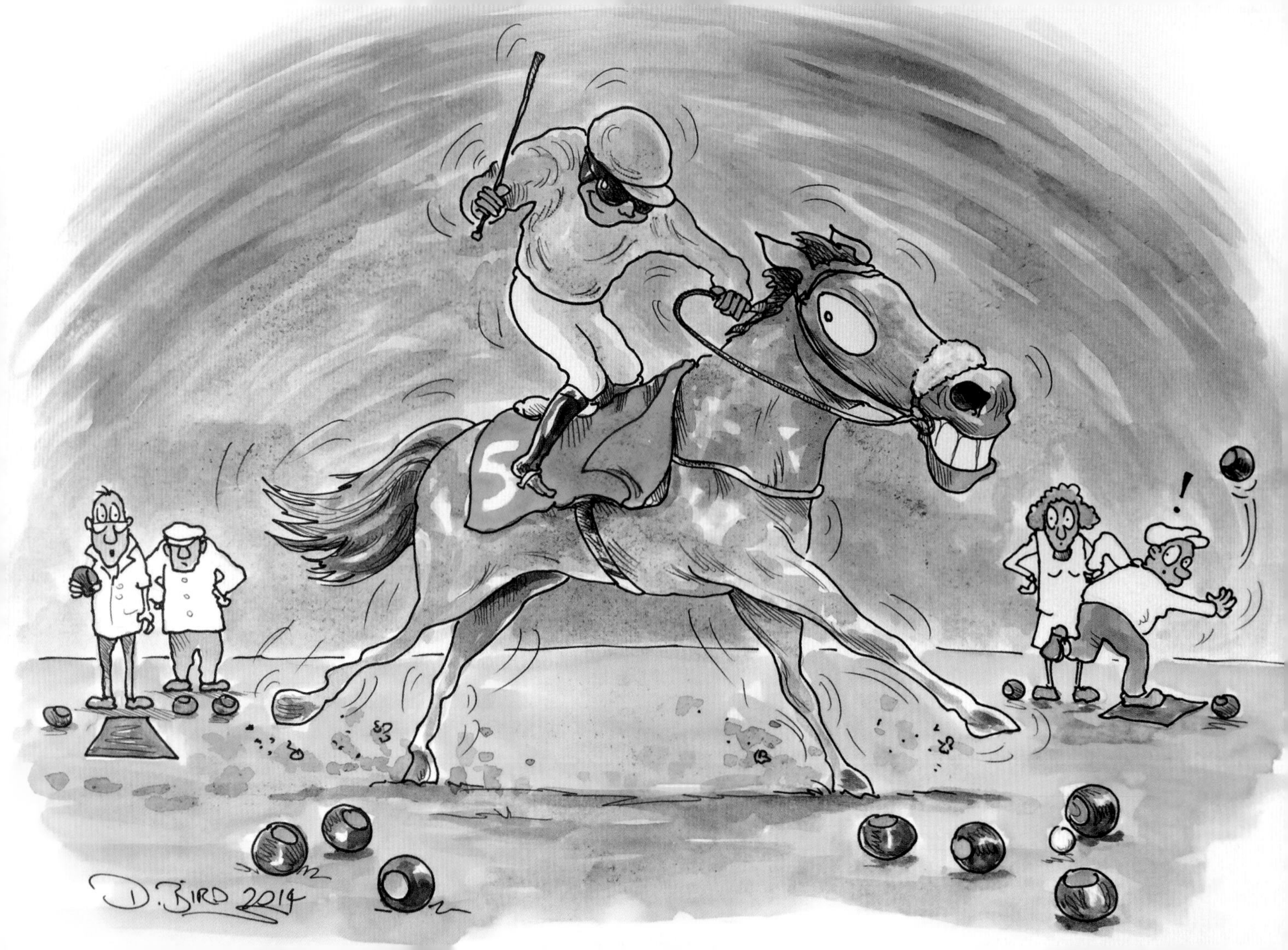
5
!
D. BIRD 2014

Grandeur runs in the Bowling Green
Handicap at Belmont Park, New York

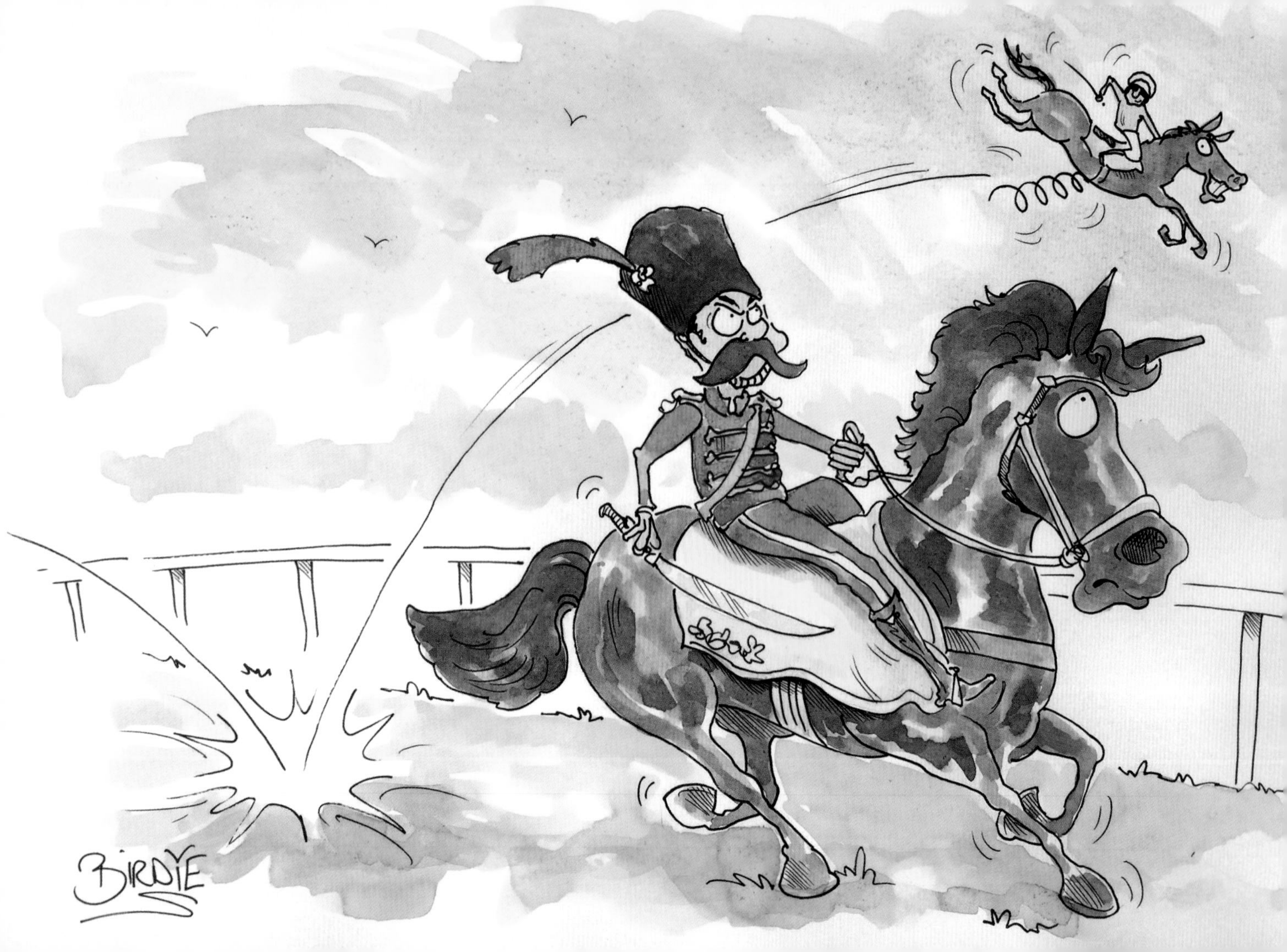
BIRDIE

Arab Spring tries to take the Brigadier Gerard Stakes at Sandown – he got beaten a head

French Navy sinks his rivals in the Earl
of Sefton Stakes at Newmarket

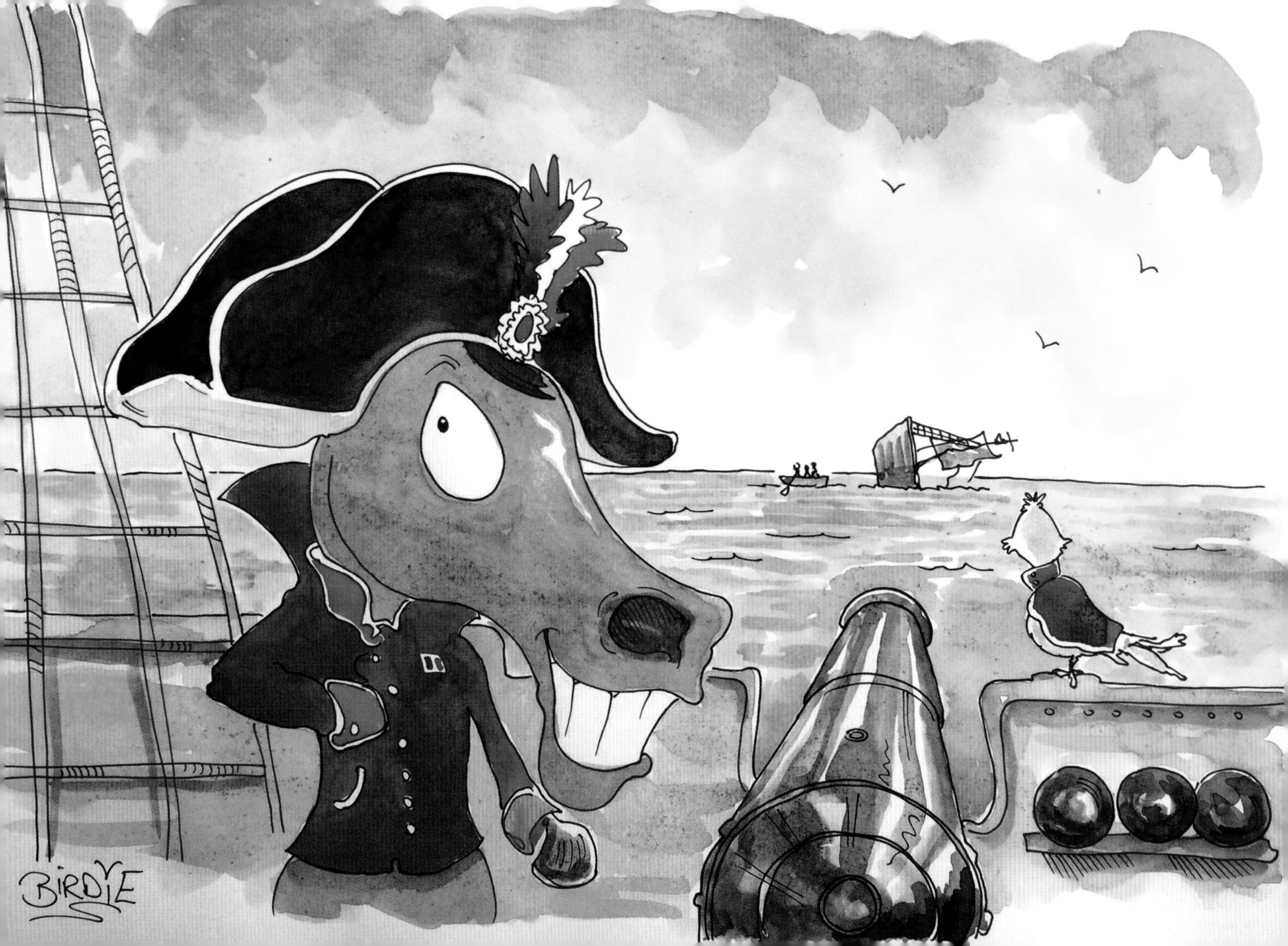
BIRDIE

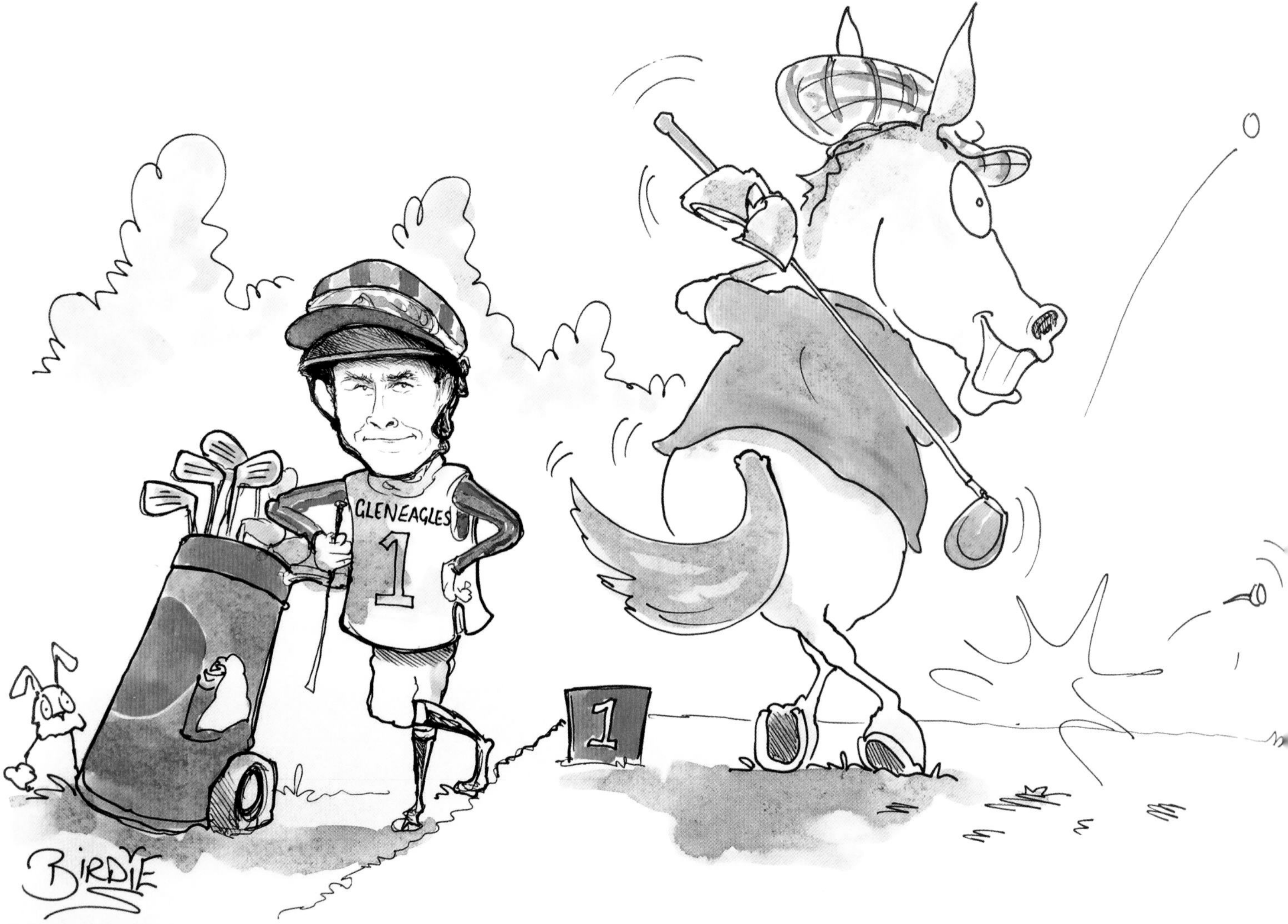
GLENEAGLES
1
1
BIRDIE

Gleneagles sends another down the fairway for caddy Ryan Moore

Abbey Road. Top NH trainers David Pipe, Paul Nicholls, Nigel Twiston-Davies, Nicky Henderson and Jonjo O'Neill re-enact the Beatles crossing

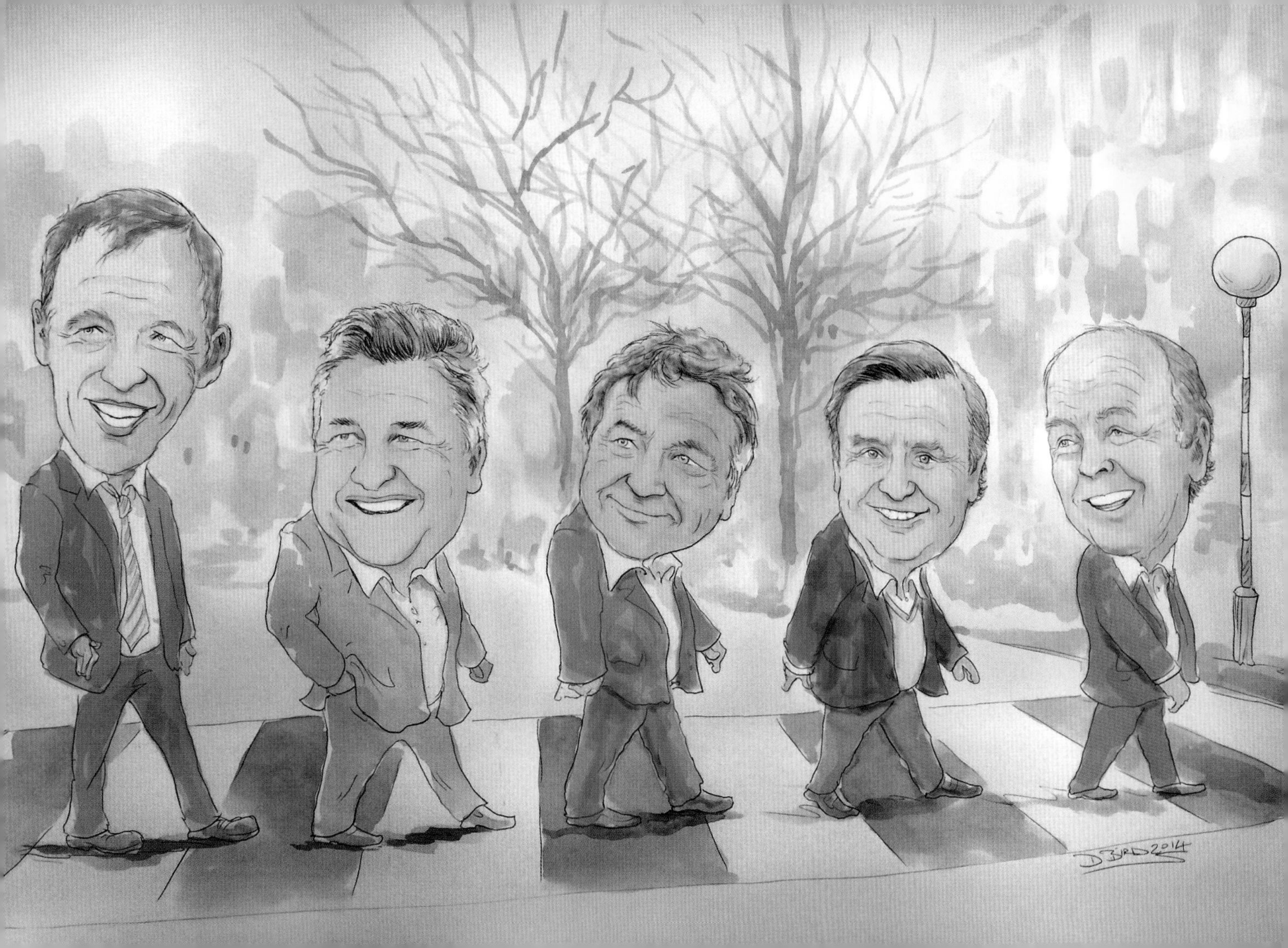
D BYRD 2014

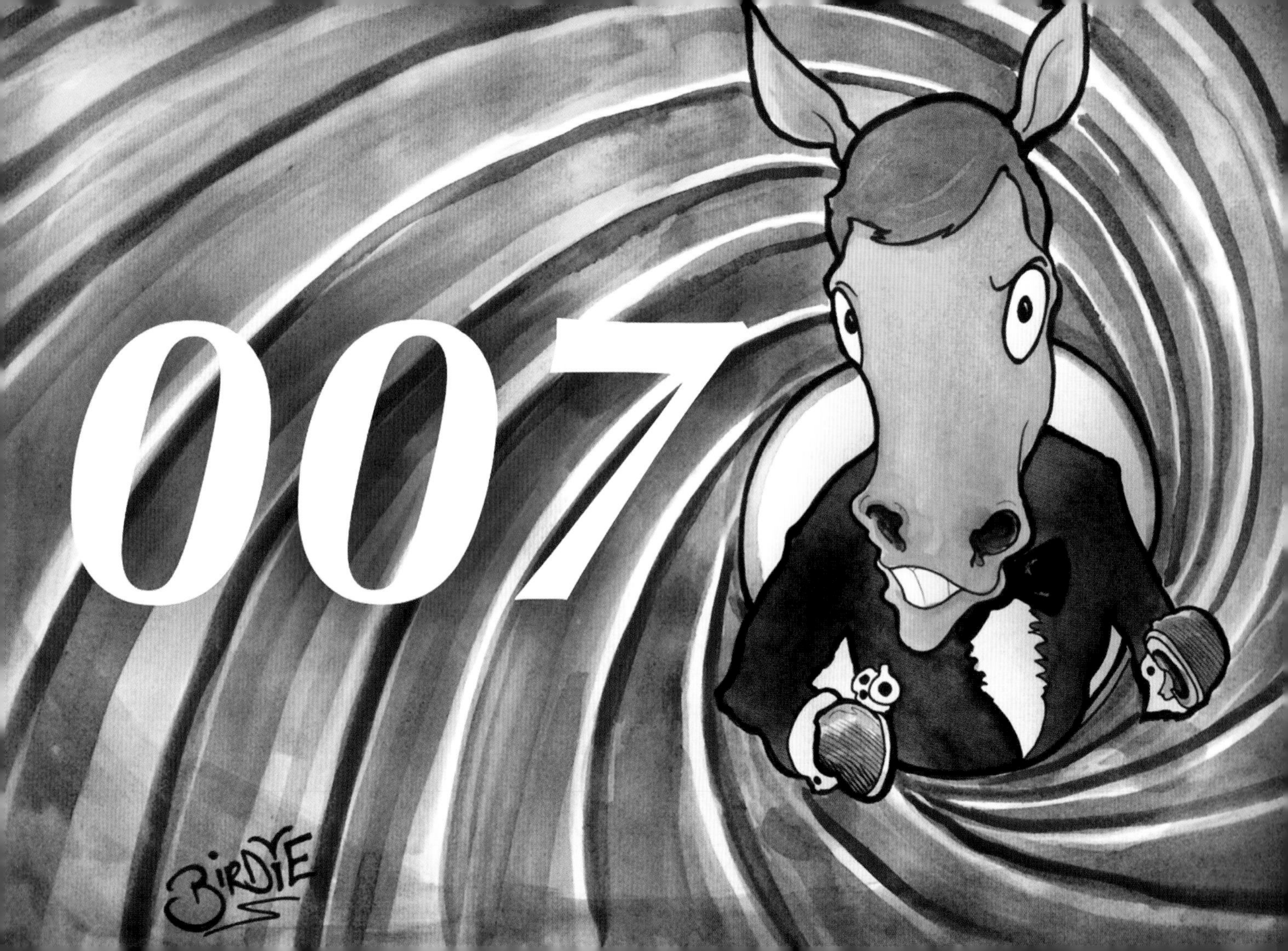
007
BIRDIE

The horse Sir Roger Moore prepares to run at
Royal Ascot, the real Sir Roger re-tweeted this!

'Miss. My daddy's here' – after his retirement,
AP has time for the school run

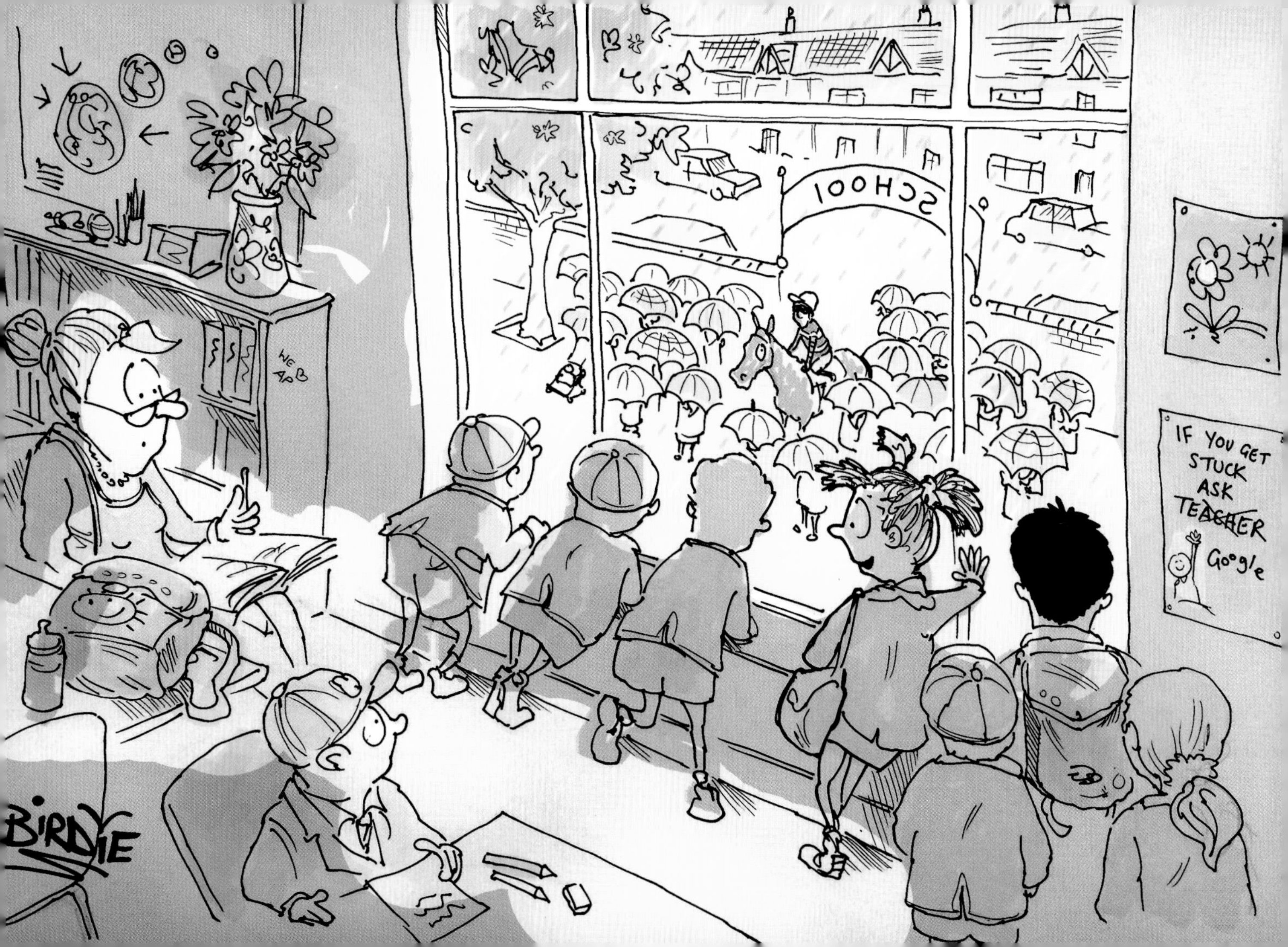
SCHOOL
IF YOU GET STUCK ASK ~~TEACHER~~ Google
BIRDIE

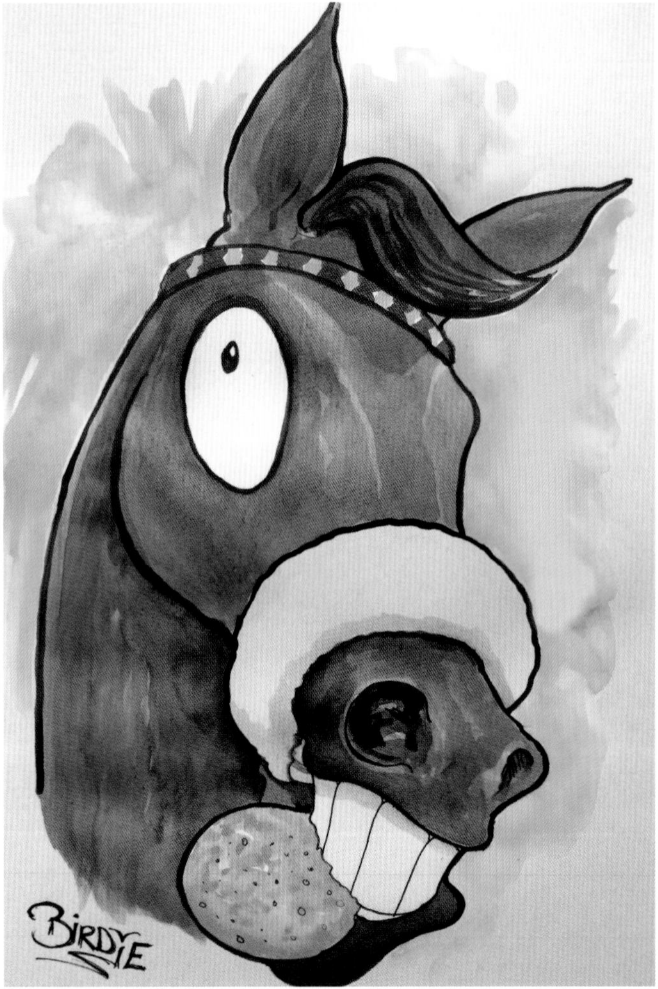
BIRDIE

Clever Cookie wins the
Ormonde Stakes at Chester

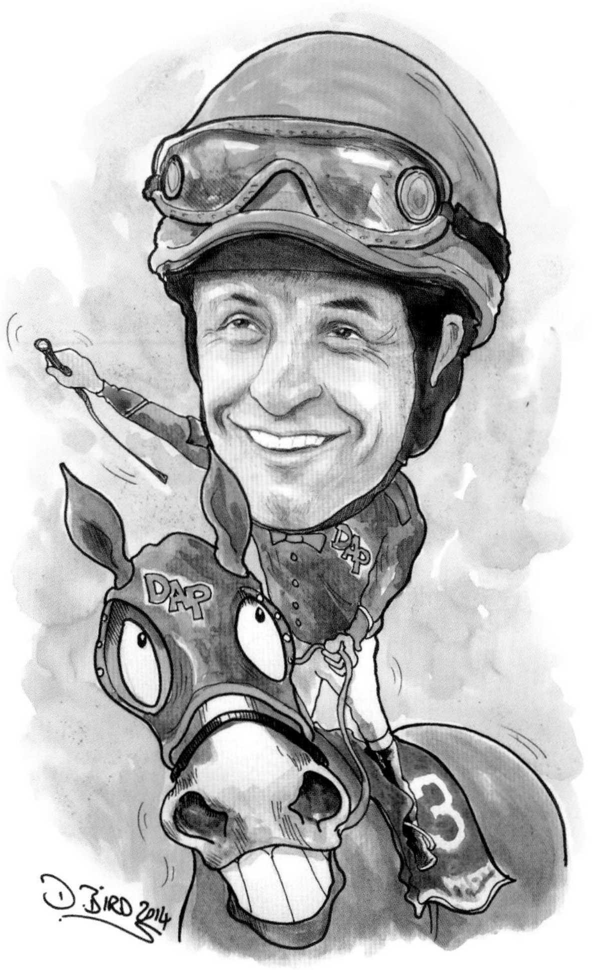
DAP
DAP
3
D. BIRD 2014

California Chrome tilts for America's Triple Crown in the Belmont Stakes – this cartoon was used in the official racecard

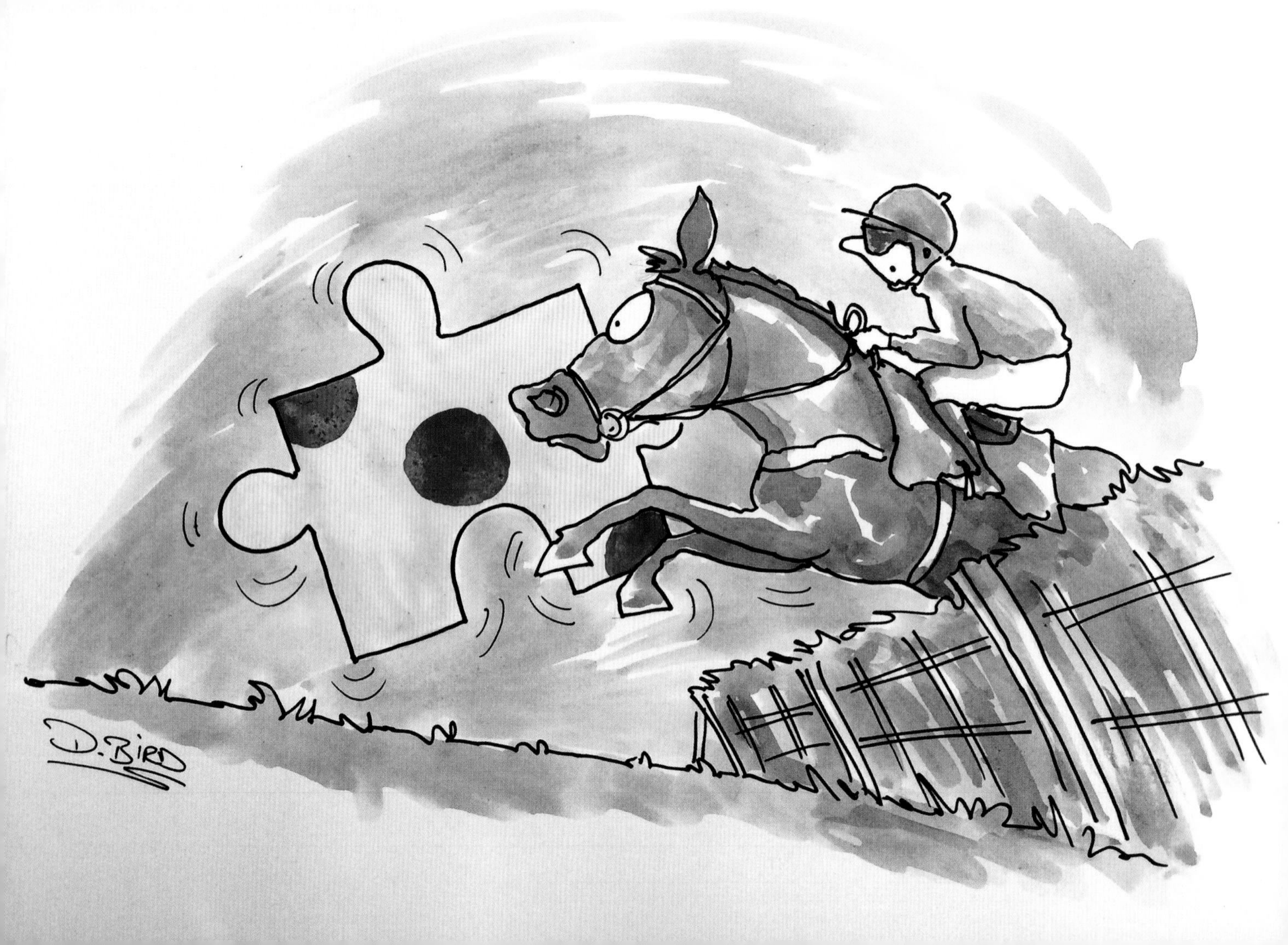
D. BIRD

Bitofapuzzle completes a successful
trip to Ireland at Fairyhouse

Cheltenham Festival 2015 sees the first ever Birdie mural –
stretching 40 feet across the new grandstand

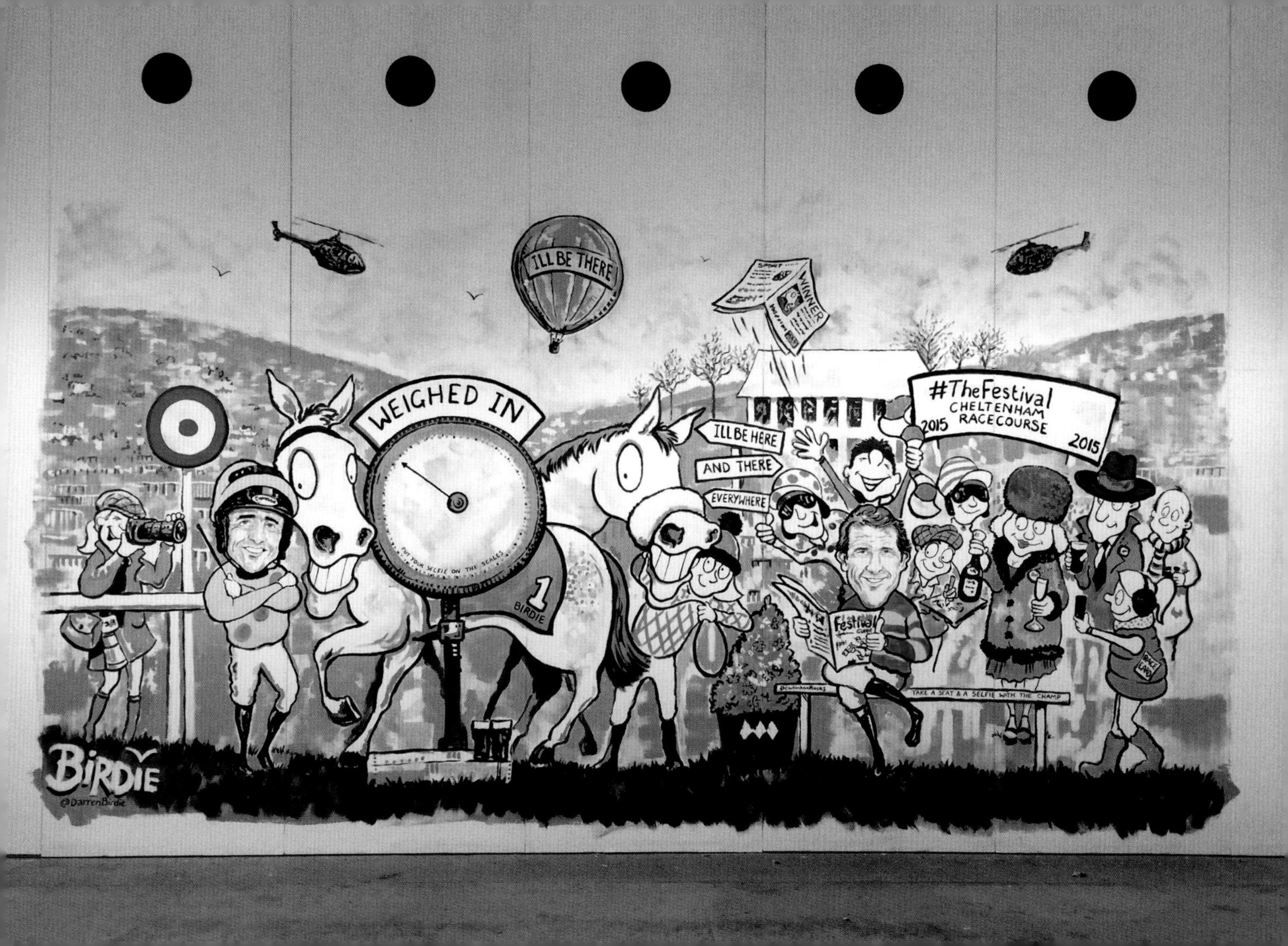
ILL BE THERE
SPORT
WINNER
WEIGHED IN
PUT YOUR SELFIE ON THE SCALES
1
BIRDIE
ILL BE HERE
AND THERE
EVERYWHERE
#TheFestival
CHELTENHAM
RACECOURSE
2015
2015
Festival
TAKE A SEAT & A SELFIE WITH THE CHAMP
BIRDIE
@DarrenBirdie

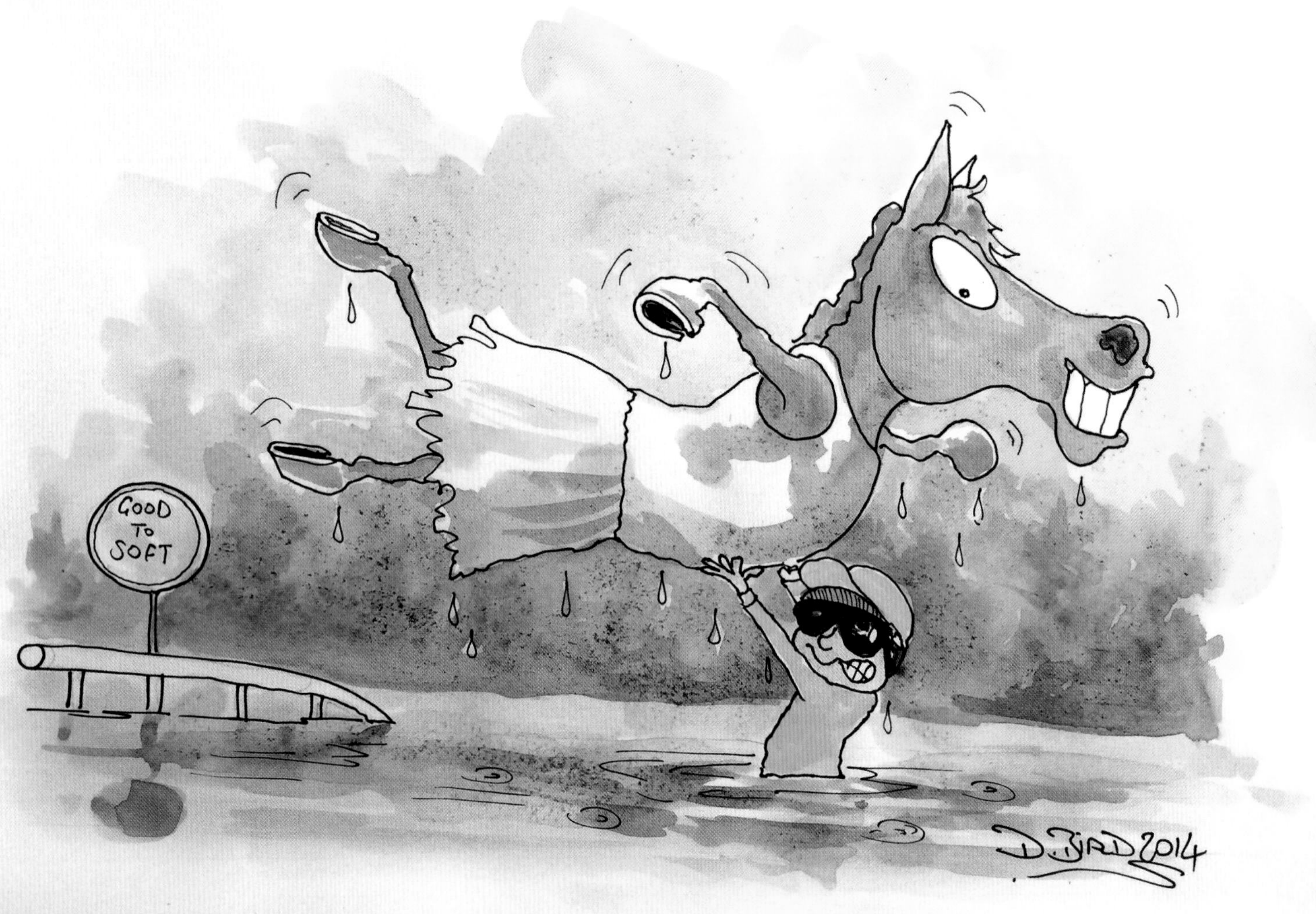
GOOD
TO
SOFT
D. BIRD 2014

Another Fine Mess on the starting rostrum

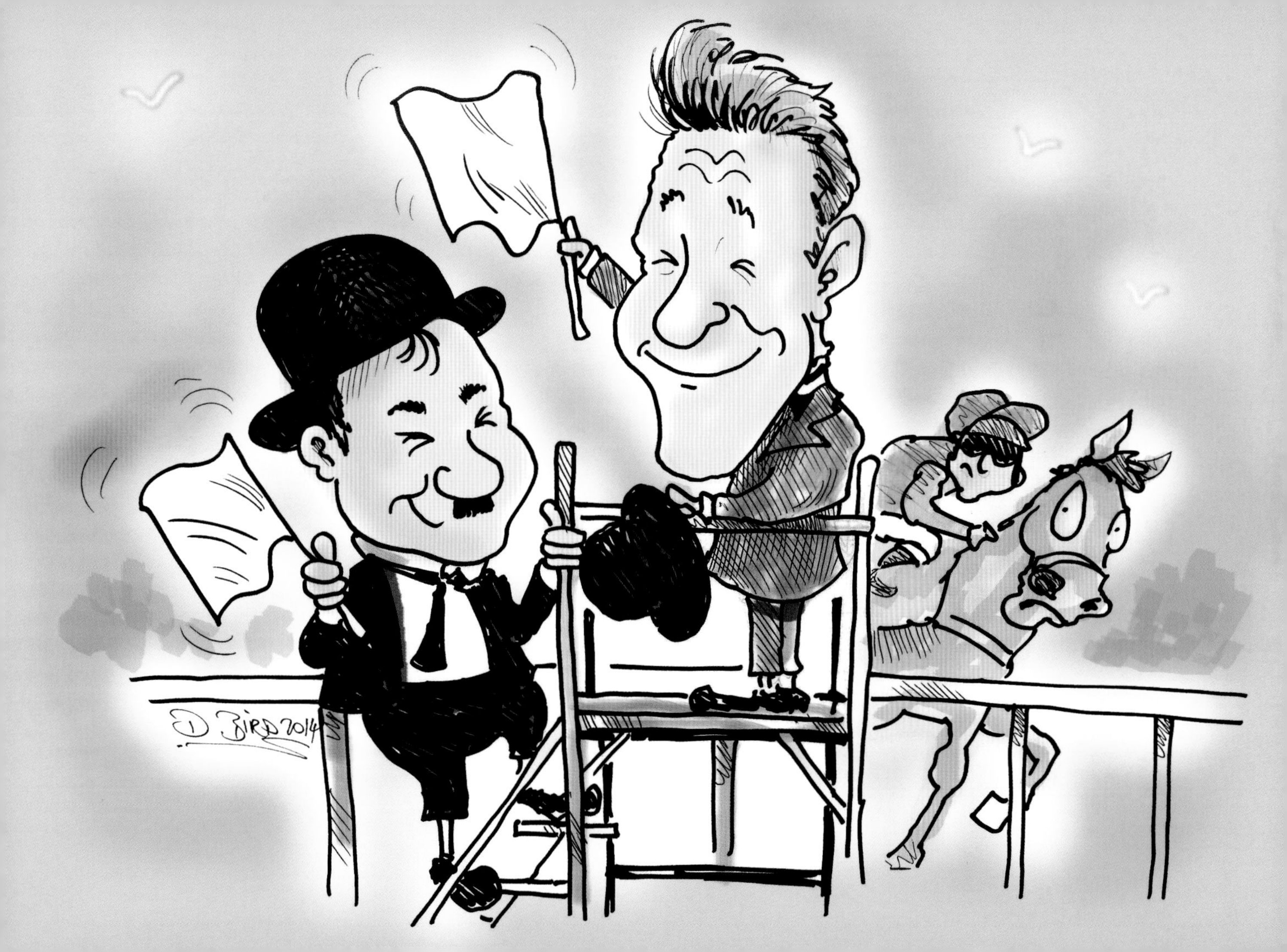
D BIRD 2014

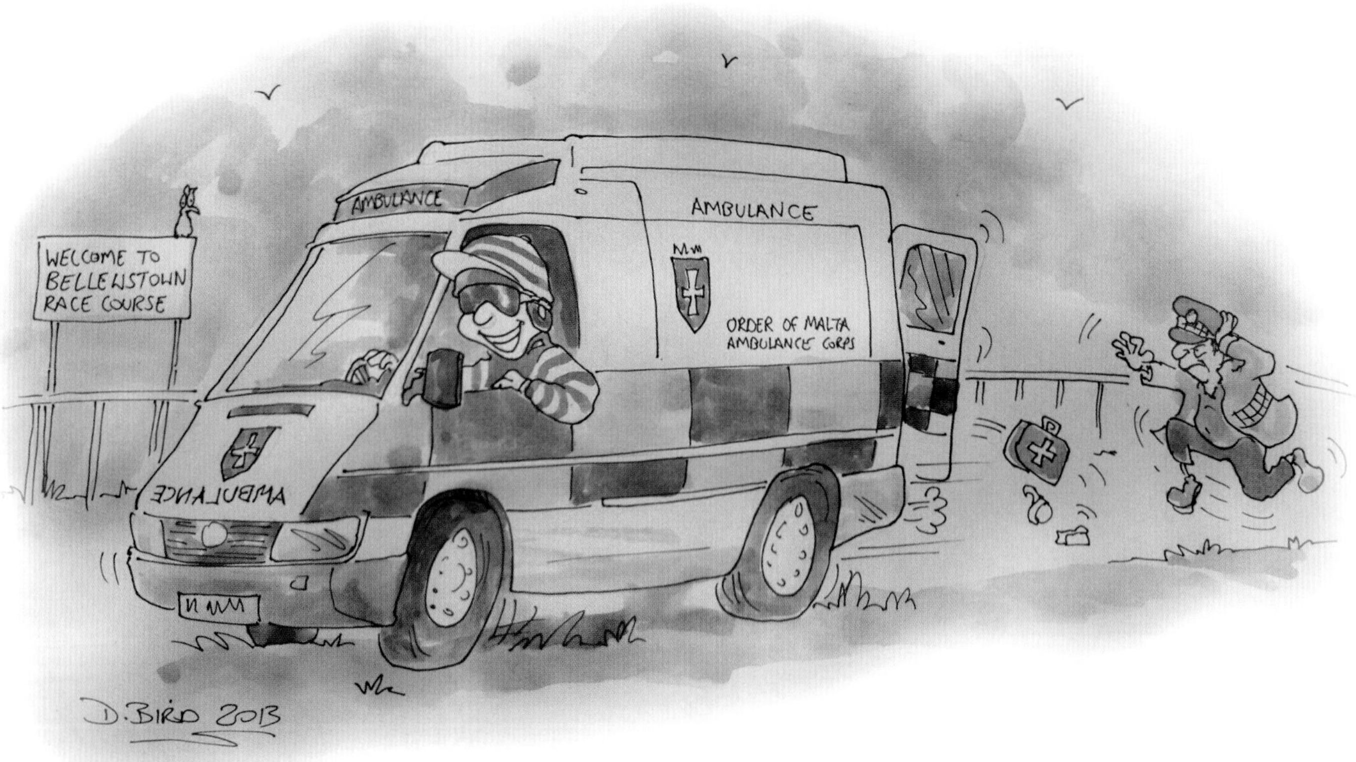
WELCOME TO
BELLEWSTOWN
RACE COURSE
AMBULANCE
AMBULANCE
ORDER OF MALTA
AMBULANCE CORPS
D. BIRD 2013

Danny Mullins hijacks an ambulance to get back to the weighing room, Bellewstown Races 2013

Super champion – Ruby Walsh on Hurricane Fly, winner of a record 22 Grade One hurdles

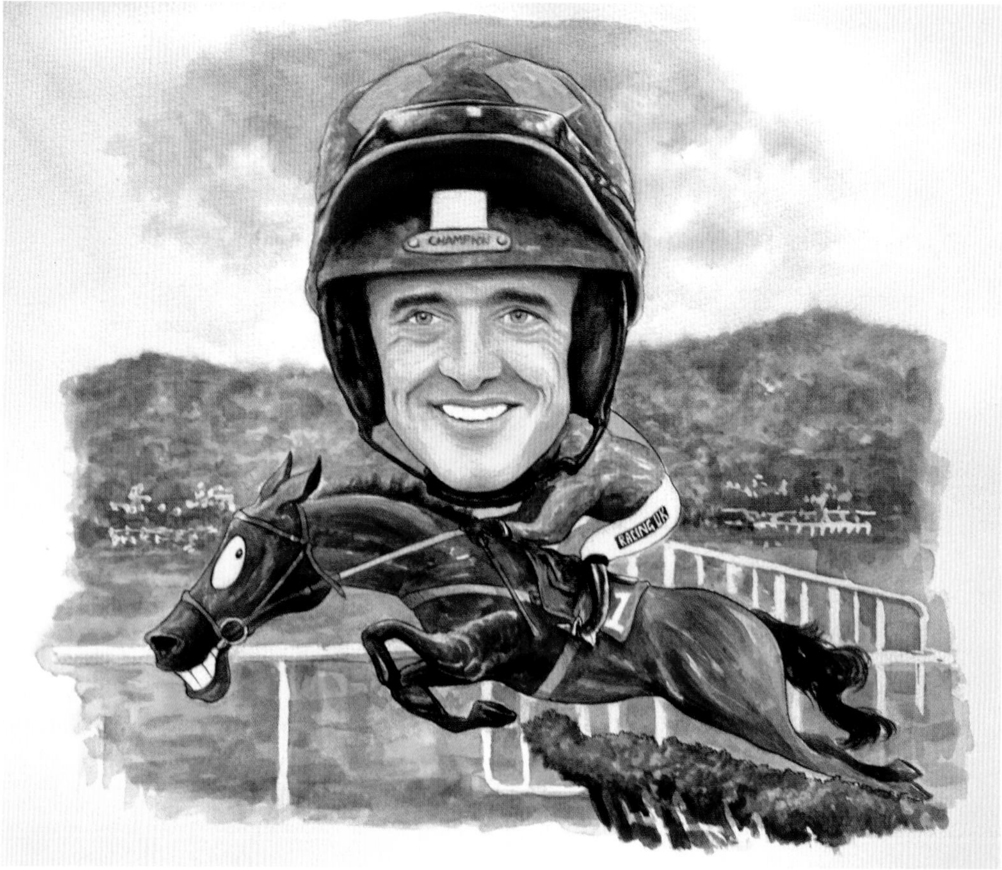
CHAMPION
RACING UK
1

Opposite: Jezki once again goes toe to toe with Hurricane Fly

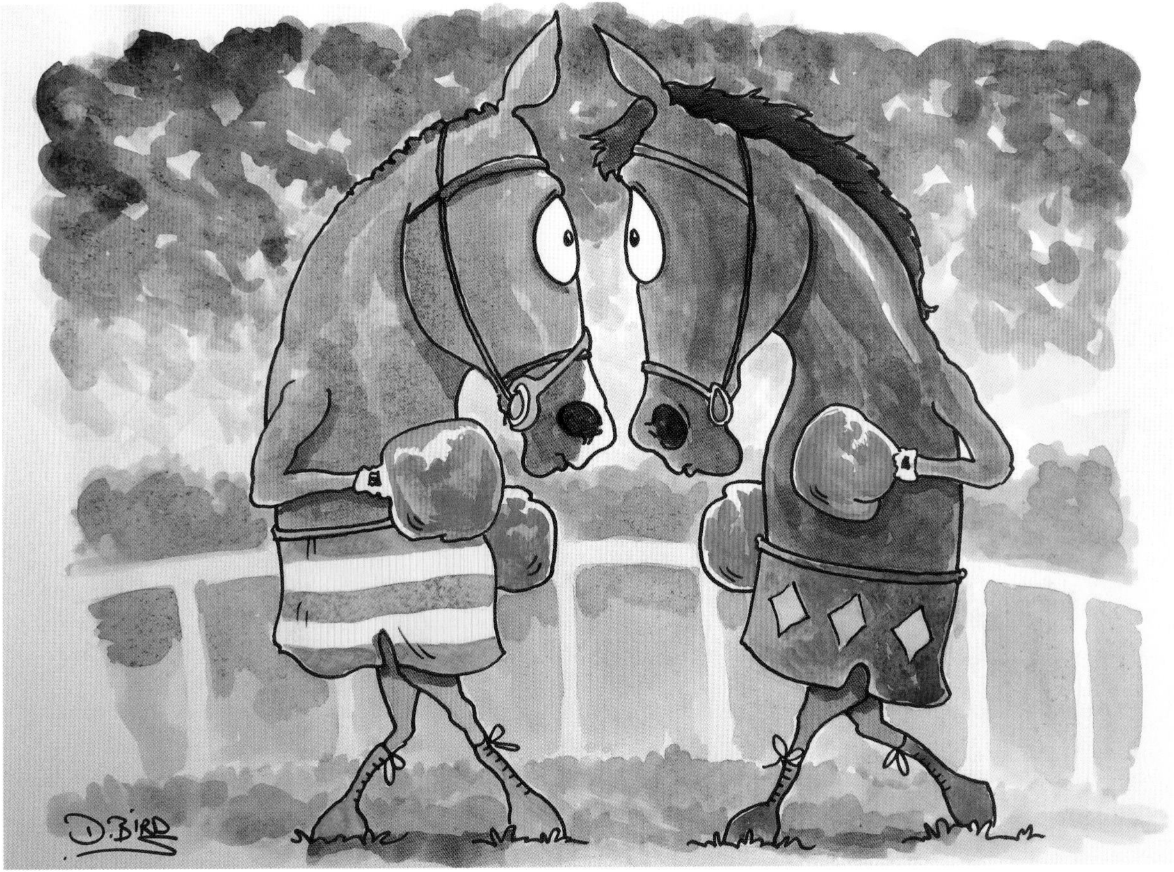
D. BIRD

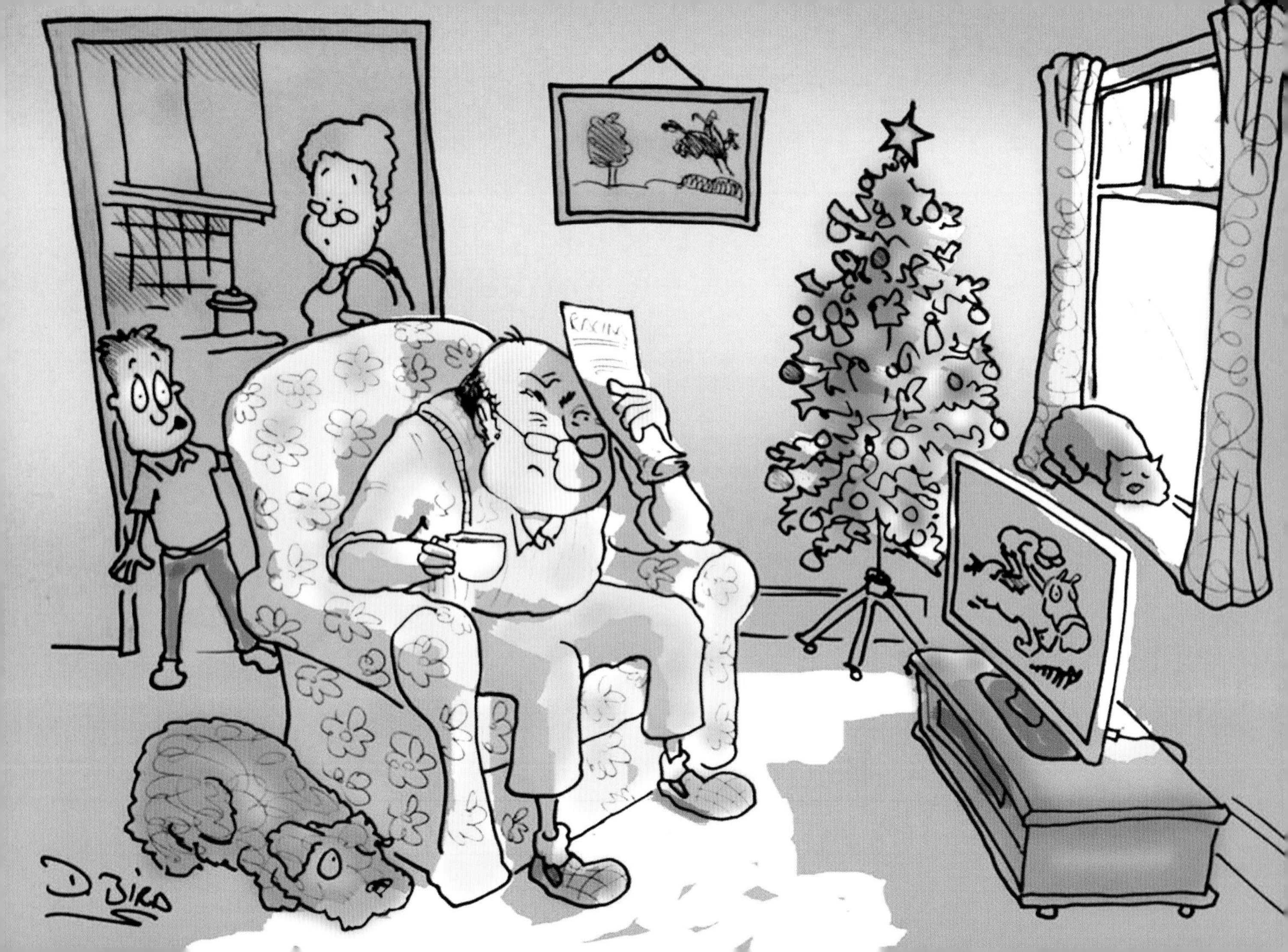
D. BIRD

'Poor old grandad, he's really blinded by the sun' – jockeys insist on omitting fences because of the low winter sun

Plenty of craic

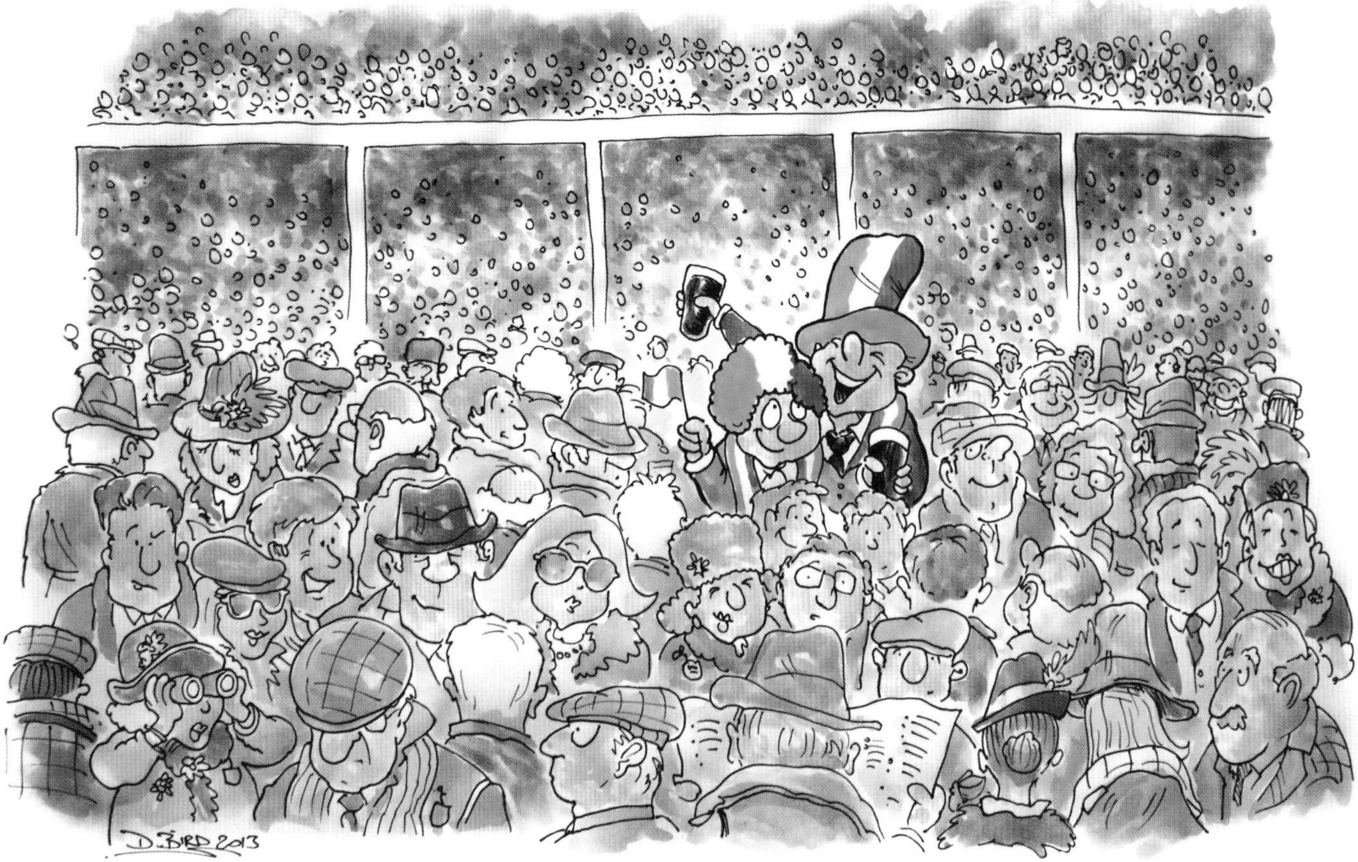
D. BIRD 2013

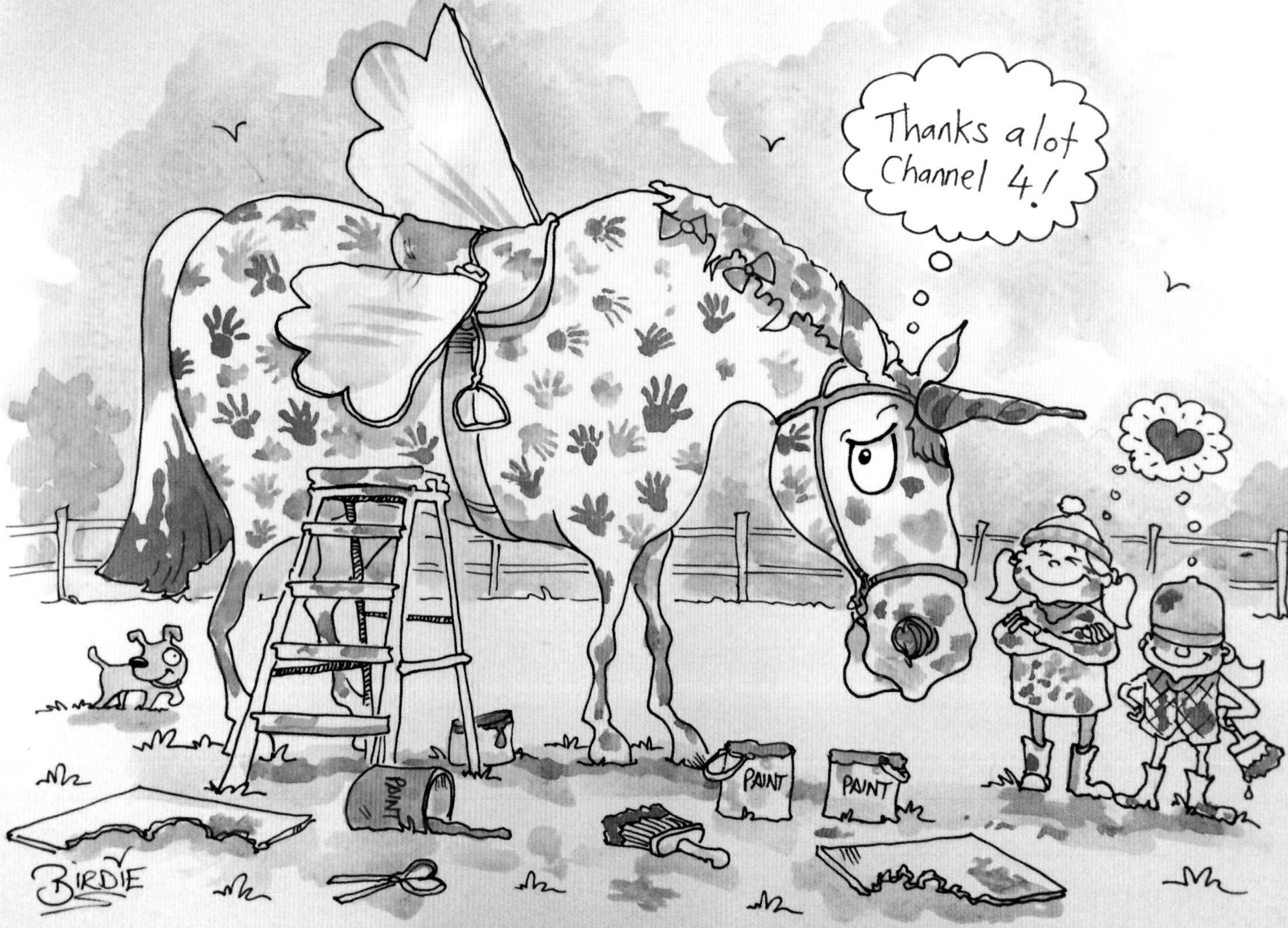
Thanks a lot Channel 4!
PAINT
PAINT
PAINT
BIRDIE

Channel 4's 2015 Grand National promotion features a unicorn

Pat Smullen wins the Irish Oaks
on Covert Love

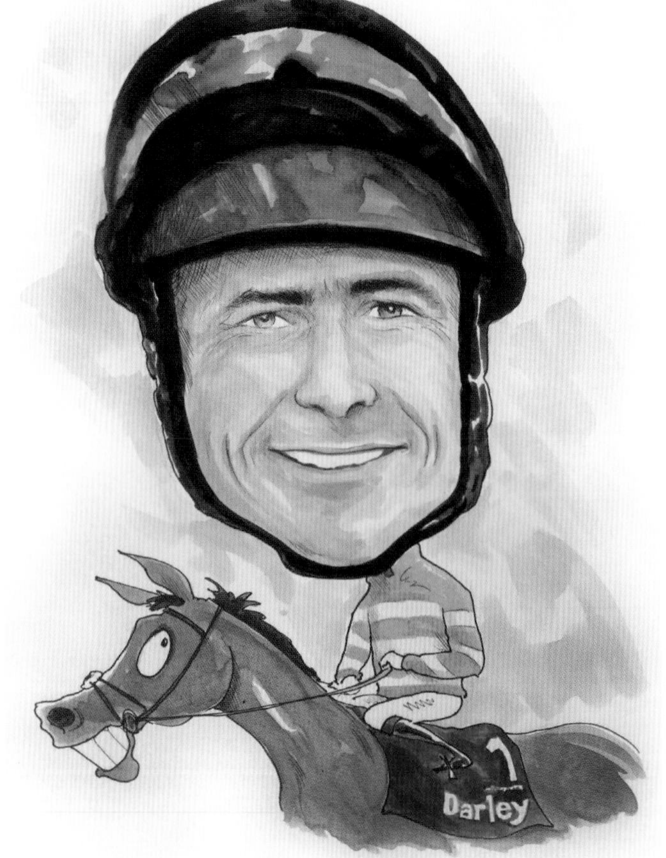
1
Darley

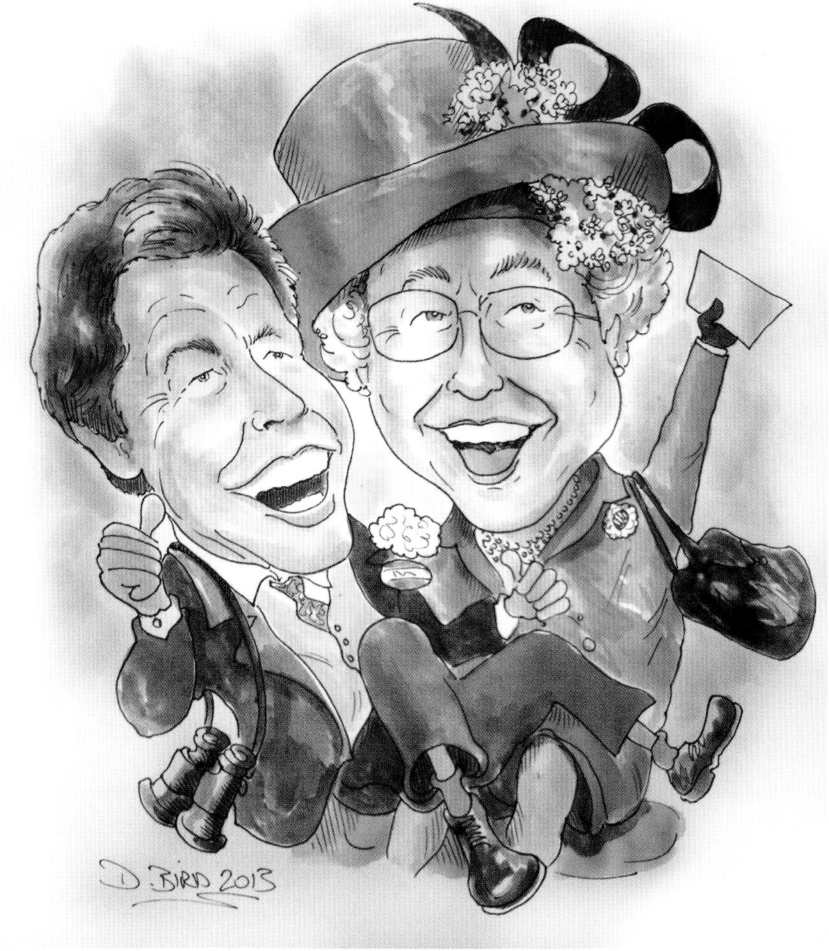
D. BIRD 2013

'Yes, we are amused' – HM The Queen and racing manager, John Warren, after Estimate's victory in the 2013 Gold Cup at Royal Ascot

'He's good with a flag' – Ruby Walsh had saved the day directing
Grand National horses around the Canal Turn at Aintree 2015

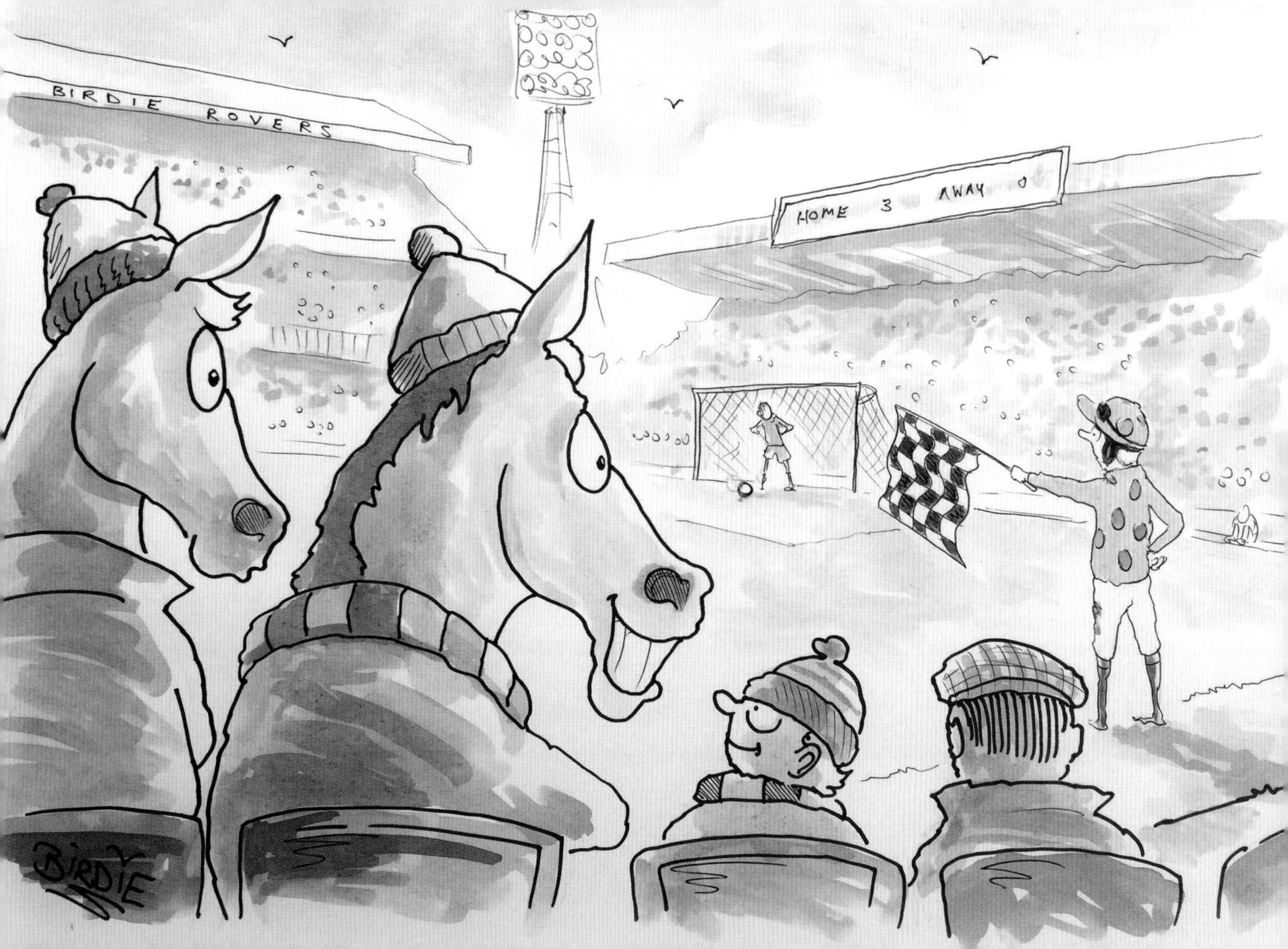
BIRDIE ROVERS
HOME 3 AWAY 0
BIRDIE

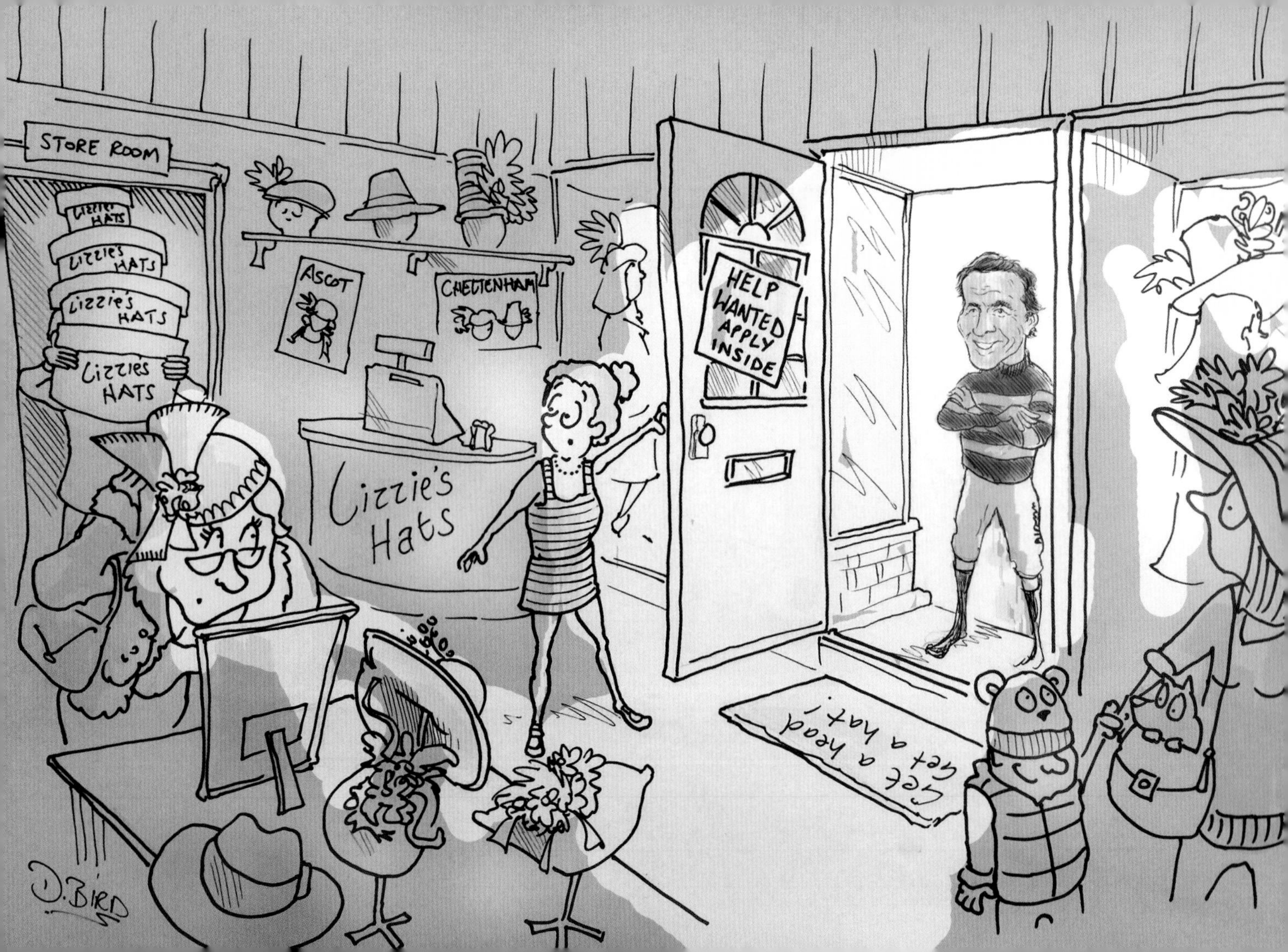
STORE ROOM
Lizzie's HATS
Lizzie's HATS
Lizzies HATS
ASCOT
CHELTENHAM
HELP WANTED APPLY INSIDE
Lizzie's Hats
Get a head get a hat!
D. BIRD

AP McCoy looks for a job in retirement

Michael Owen's Brown Panther misbehaves on his first visit to Canada

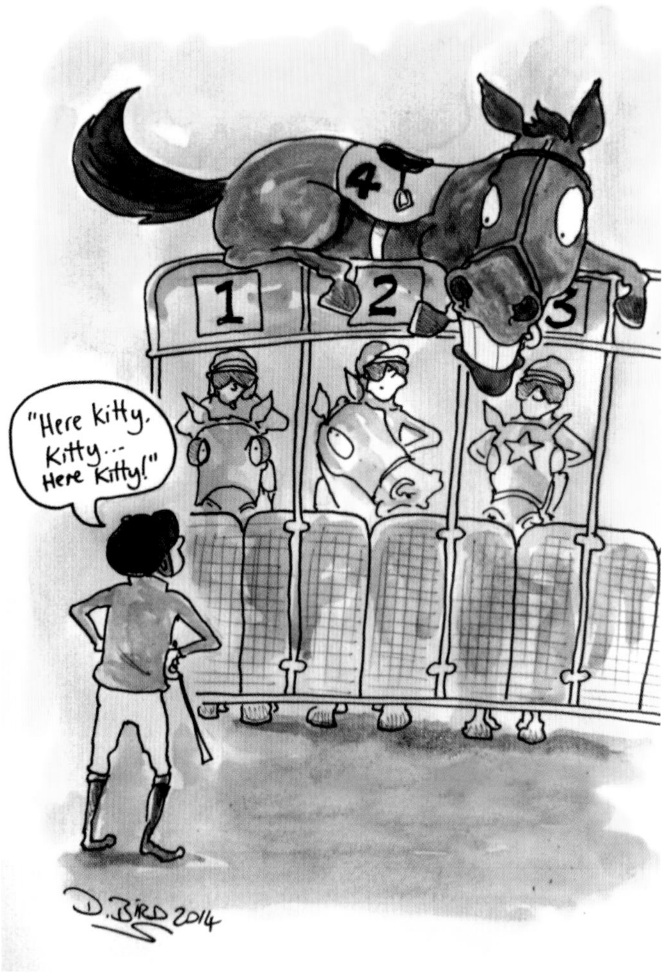
"Here kitty, kitty... Here kitty!"
1
2
3
4
D. BIRD 2014

Big Orange wins the Goodwood Cup

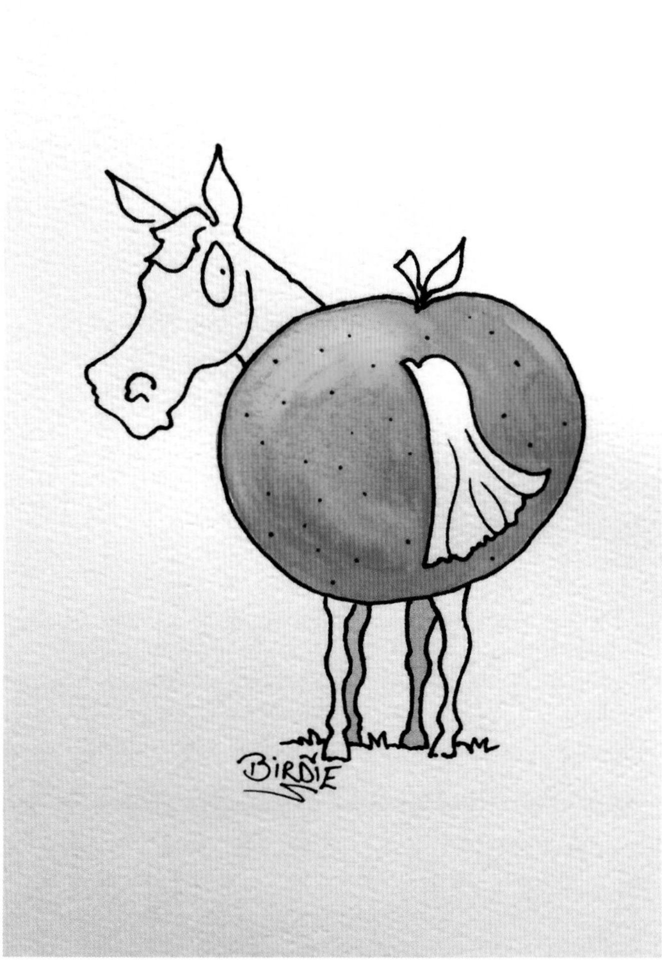
BIRDIE

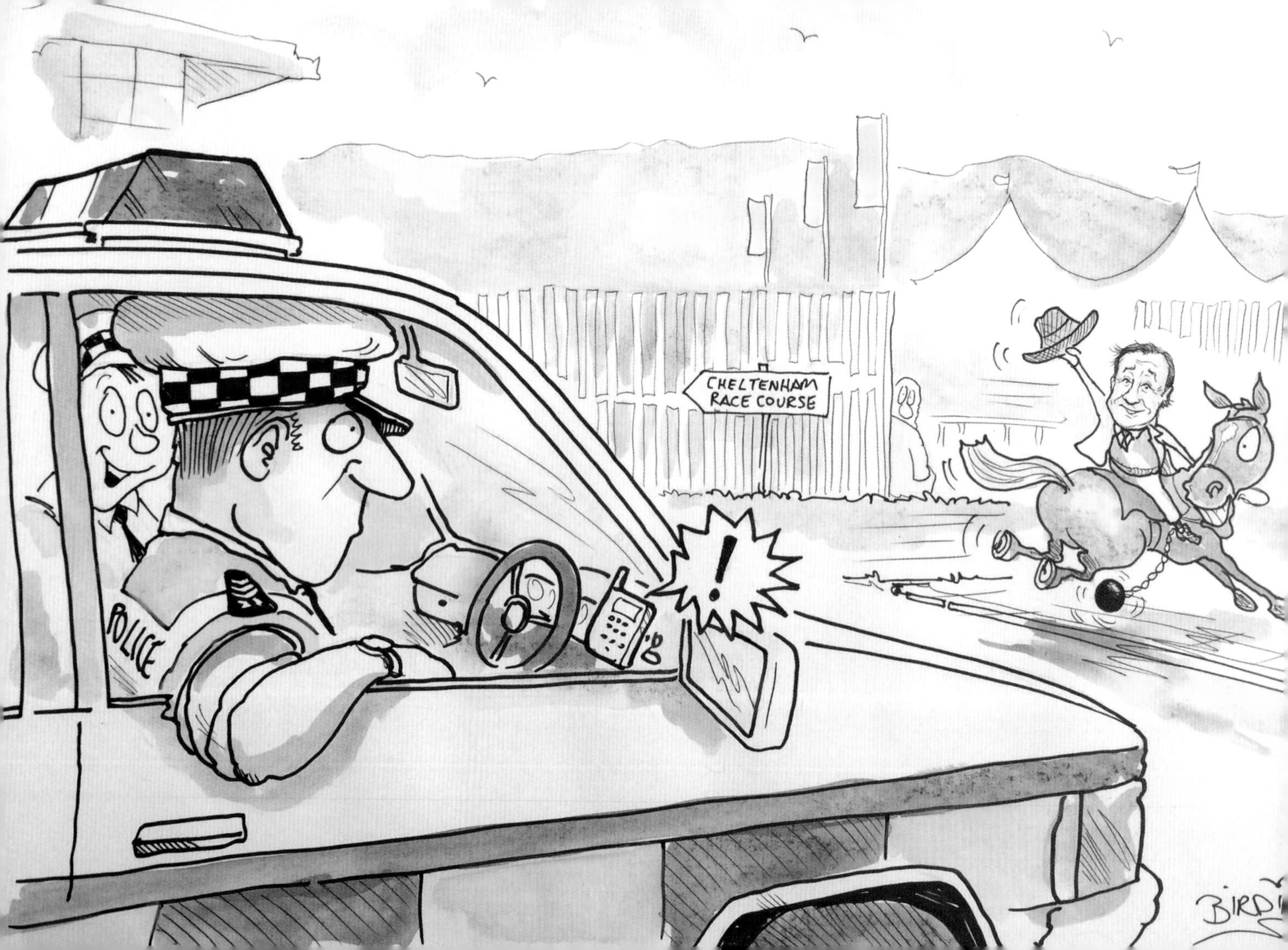
CHELTENHAM
RACE COURSE
POLICE
!

Nicky Henderson's Call The Cops wins at the Cheltenham Festival

'He'll ruin my good looks' says Pat Smullen after Parish Hall tries to bite him in a finish at the Curragh

© Caroline Norris

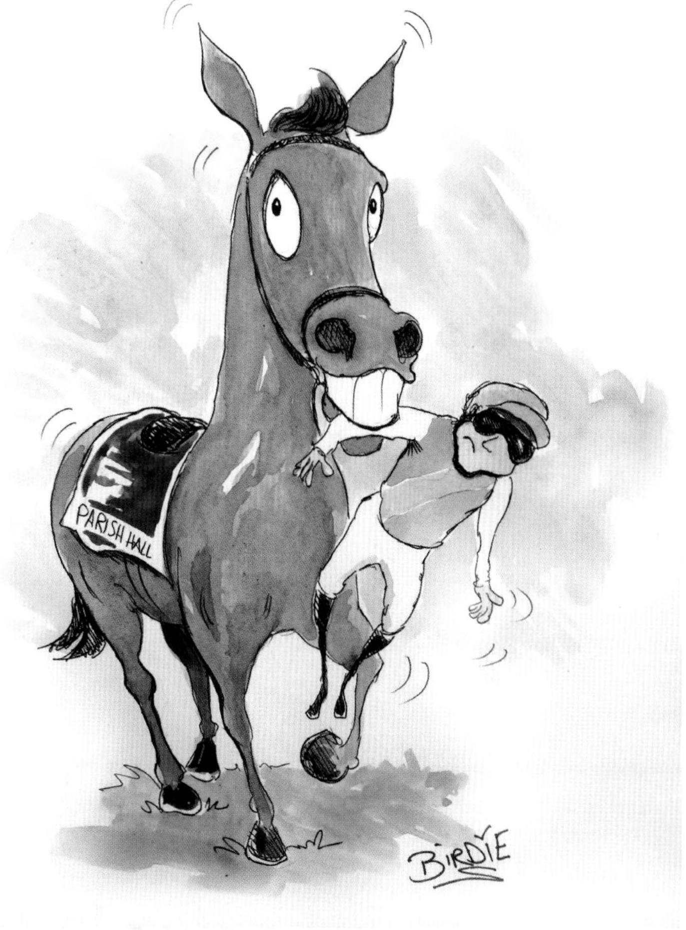
PARISH HALL
BIRDIE

Luke Harvey and Jason Weaver on Attheraces –
this was the first cartoon that Birdie ever tweeted

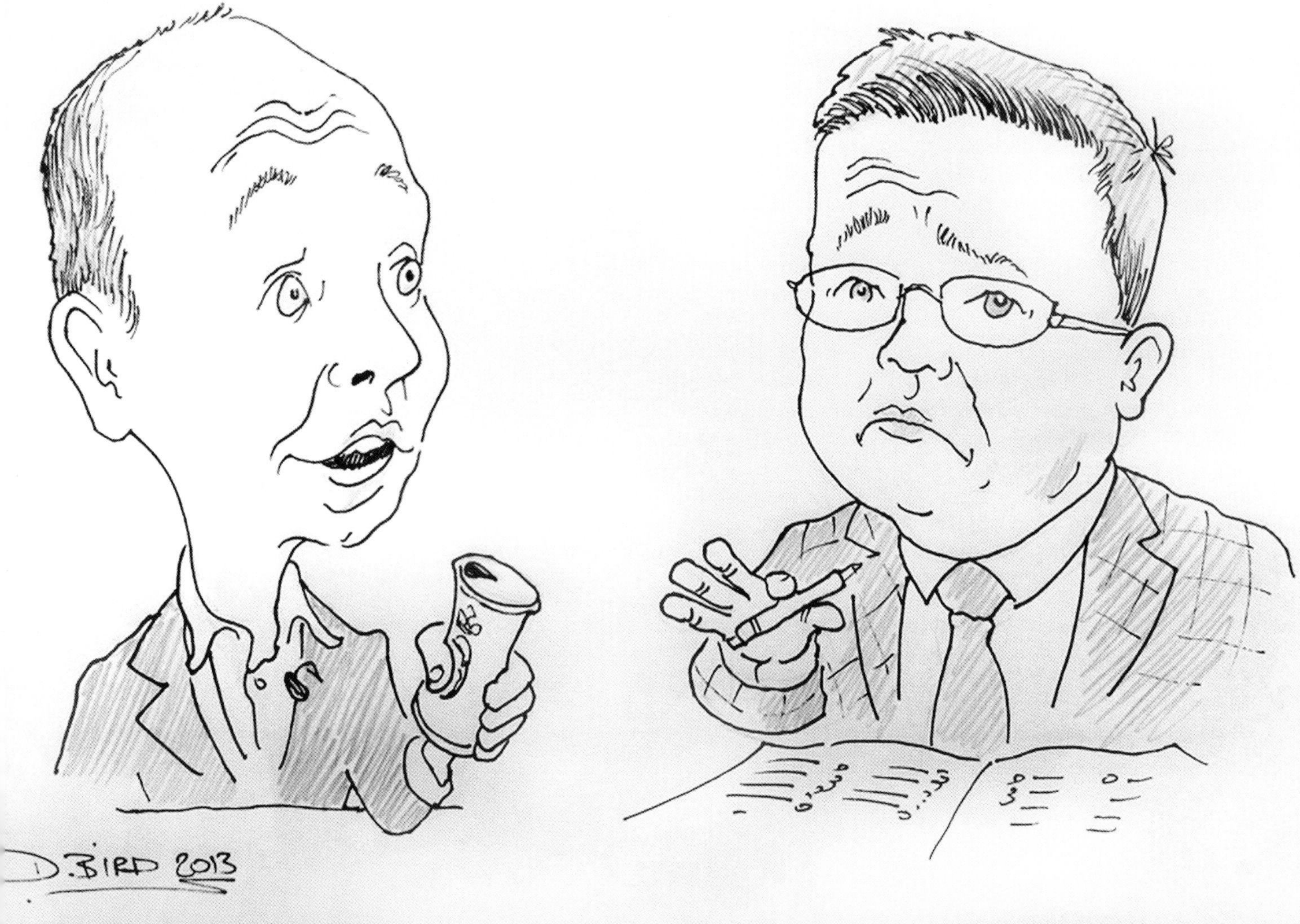
D.BIRD 2013

My journey began on a Friday evening in 2013 when I tweeted my first ever racing cartoon to the 'Get In' show on Attheraces. The five minute sketch of show hosts Luke Harvey and Jason Weaver was just a bit of fun but within a few minutes it suddenly appeared on my TV screen! And 'Birdie' was born...

Channel 4 Racing invited me to appear on The Morning Line show at the 2014 Cheltenham Festival. I sketched live on air each day of the festival creating images of the presenters and guests. Mick Fitzgerald was the first person to shake my hand on day one and I found myself surrounded by other racing celebrities and heroes of the sport I love.

I'd like therefore to give a special mention to Luke, Jason and all the ATR team and Mick and all the Channel 4 team. Your support has been so very appreciated.

I would like to thank Racing Post Books for the opportunity to publish my first 'Birdie' book and especially Brough Scott for his belief and enthusiasm in me.

Special thanks also to Liz Ampairee and Julian Brown for devoting so much of their time and efforts towards making this book a reality.

Last, but definitely not least, I'd like to thank all of my followers on social media and the racing community as a whole. Their enjoyment of my work has helped me to pursue the cartoon dreams of Darren 'Birdie' Bird!